BY ROBERT KELLY

Armed Descent (1961)
Her Body Against Time (1963)
Round Dances (1964)
Enstasy (1964)
Lunes (1964)
Lectiones (1965)
Words In Service (1965)
Weeks (1966)
The Scorpions (1967)
Song XXIV (1967)
Devotions (1967)
Twenty Poems (1967)
Axon Dendron Tree (1967)
Crooked Bridge Love Society (1967)
A Joining (1967)
Alpha (1968)
Finding the Measure (1968)
Sonnets (1968)
Statement (1968)
Songs I-XXX (1968)
The Common Shore (1969)
A California Journal (1969)
Kali Yuga (1970)
Cities (1971)
In Time (1971)
Flesh Dream Book (1971)
Ralegh (1972)
The Pastorals (1972)
Reading Her Notes (1972)
The Tears of Edmund Burke (1973)
The Mill of Particulars (1973)
A Line of Sight (1974)
The Loom (1975)
Sixteen Odes (1976)
The Lady Of (1977)
The Convections (1978)
Wheres (1978)
The Book of Persephone (1978)
The Cruise of the Pnyx (1979)
Kill the Messenger Who Brings Bad News (1979)

Editor

A Controversy of Poets (1965)

Robert Kelly

KILL THE MESSENGER

BLACK SPARROW PRESS

WHO BRINGS BAD NEWS

Kill the messenger
who brings bad news—
the world is only
description

ANTA BARBARA 1979

ACKNOWLEDGEMENT

These poems were composed in 1976 and 1977. Some few of them appeared in magazines, whose editors I thank now for the permission to reprint: *Text* (Mark Karlins and Bruce McClelland), *Flute* (Brian McInerny), *Alcheringa* (Dennis Tedlock and Barbara Tedlock), *Paideuma* (Carroll F. Terrell), *Canto* (Pat Goodheart), *Shell* (Jack Kimball). I want to thank Noreen Norton for typing the manuscript.

Composition of these poems was encouraged by a National Endowment of the Arts fellowship for 1977, and editorial completion helped by a CAPS Grant for 1978.

LIBRARY OF CONGRESS CATALOGING IN PUBLICATION DATA

Kelly, Robert, 1935-
  Kill the messenger who brings bad news.

  I. Title.
PS3521.E4322K5   811'.5'4   79-21994
ISBN 0-87685-432-3 (paper edition)
ISBN 0-87685-433-1 (signed cloth edition)

To Mary

Close close
as if a lover
had forgotten ever to withdraw

TABLE OF CONTENTS

East River / 13
Wintereve / 14
The birds told me / 15
Blond face of the refusing woman / 16
this wasted day / 17
Texts : 23 [The bird that hovers] / 18
Wanderers Nachtlied / 21
Magic Annandale / 22
The Confession / 23
Σνμμαχος εσσο / 24
The Queen of Between / 25
Garnets / 28
I would like to find a thing I can talk about / 30
Ship Burial / 32
I wish I could hold on to what the boy held onto / 35
The Beatrice / 36
The Mediatrix / 38
My lap is / 41
The Ceiba Tree of the Tzotzil / 42
The Long March / 44
The Menelaus / 45
May snow up Mead Mountain / 46
Parthenon / 47
A Woman from Connaught / 49
The Siren / 51
Lontano / 53
Dance Suite on a Phrase of D. H. Lawrence / 54
Women of the Bois de Boulogne / 59
Shiva / 65
The Traveler / 67
The Balustrade / 68
Ode on the Two Hundredth Birthday of this Commonwealth / 70
El Desdichado / 74

Quarante / 76

The Mix   /   92
Three Turkish Pictures   /   93
The Court Painter   /   102
Should Eros have   /   103
Wrang-gaites   /   105
At the Nottingham Assizes   /   107
The Blue   /   108
Sunday Morning   /   111
Andre Malraux Dying in a Paris Hospital   /   112
To contend with   /   113
A wedge in the nature of the world   /   115
Six Marian Hymns:
      Sequences of woods also   /   116
      Some know you as Mary   /   117
      And great Lucius your votary   /   118
      O you most intricate   /   119
      To the new-born of it   /   120
      Our blue words mantle you in a fur   /   121
To Aphrodite   /   122
Studies from the Mishnah:
        I. Can the shadow of a menstruating woman defile?   /   123
      III. DBR   /   125
        V. If the blood falls on his left hand it is invalid   /   127
Meditation on a well-known Phrase of St Augustine   /   129
In Florence, in Piero's Time   /   130
Surgical Piano   /   132
Of Poetics   /   133
Canto CXXX   /   134
First Jewish Sonnet   /   136
Second Jewish Sonnet   /   137
Third Jewish Sonnet   /   138
There Is a Room Where It Is Rare   /   139
Turangalila Meditation   /   141
The Archive   /   143

The Runaway Slave / 144
Texts : 32 [Hymn to Phrygian Aphrodite] / 146
My Correspondence with Hemingway / 148
The War Criminal / 151
The Missionary / 153
*The Table Drank the Milk / 157
tell me love how bodies pray / 159
Let the Nobody who cares / 160
Gypsies / 161
Not I think what I / 162
Texts : 25 [The Philosopher's Stone] / 163
Arctic Embryo / 168

Easter / 169

The Agony in the Garden / 179
Blue Nude / 181
The Woman Who Heard Horses Scream at Dusk / 184
mazy moon / 185
At the well bent low / 186
The Talk of Angels / 187
The Devotees / 189
Day 5-Quiej / 190

Early Spring Day Along the Housatonic / 192

The Ones / 199
Casting / 201
Ghazal / 203
Seven cities / 204
A Book of Solutions / 205
Swallowtail / 206
Tannhäuser / 210
The Shortstop / 213

The Trial / 214
A New Ecology / 217
The Shield of Achilles / 218
Her Name / 220
This Earth a Necklace Bead for Whom / 221
You Are In Water / 222
The Lover / 223
The Goddess / 225
The Visit / 227
Portrait of a Man Alone / 228
The Dismembered / 229
Virgil / 230
The Place / 231
"Queen of Heaven" Variations / 232
Herod / 234
INRI / 235
Seeds / 236
The holy mist / 237
The Death of Lenny Bruce / 240
It is Always a Matter of Return / 241
Say good morning to the earliest machine / 242

KILL THE MESSENGER WHO BRINGS BAD NEWS

East River

Did he have enough breath to
and saying it did the dimple
where a drop of rain preserved her image
still twinkle in his otherwise dusty mind?
Subways led to her, so he loved cities.
How deep the river is, cold, fangoso,
bottom gluey with old cars, bones, bibles
if he went down there would open to a text
from the Song of Songs about his heavy shoes
and how he drags himself to the Beloved
where the river flows into the Lower Bay.
The dust dissolved. The list of all the foods
he had ever had for breakfast
unrolls like music, baroque, mechanic,
as he tries to focus on the layers of salt and sweet.
She comes from a joining or *she lives*
where rivers join. But are they these
rivers, this joining? Foods left over
from last night are infinite.
She must be something he ate,
that dropped out of memory's dingy cigar box
when a pink rubberband snapped and his loves
all tumbled together, input and output
confused, face upon face. Maybe
the bottle green thick cold river will
wash the mess away. North Atlantic green
beautiful cold common water. He could remember
when he was a child he prayed to it.

Wintereve

There is nothing but this purple landscape
fell down on us from the hump-backed moon

at the middle of a month, a mouth
under a mountain.

Wives yearn with eyes & mice & crows
across this river topped with blades of ice

too thin to walk on, too slow, too slow.
There is an hysterical logic of winter nights

quiet women afraid of their porches,
their spruces blue in moonlight. I too am afraid

that I am really here, that this shadow on the snow
is my own weltering eternal shadow

that the birds fly past with ice in their beaks
& this place is my place.

≡

The birds told me
some
by going some by staying

Blond face of the refusing woman
more beautiful than any welcome.

It was "The Garden of the Finzi-Continis,"
the girl was tender, would not

make love with her like,
she said, because love in that sad

half-overgrown garden was an exile,
love was an exile

& never knew the beauty of itself
close in the dreary leaves.

Enough of the movie. Refusal,
what does refusal mean

that her face acquires such a deep
look, as if even a non-lover

could stare into it for hours
watching the faint wind of her feelings

focus. Love means to find
your original religion, to be sent

out of your garden, your country,
to die for it & never be sure.

≡

this wasted day
nothing
but this

The bird that hovers
over the text,
        a falcon
      motionless
          above the man,
'to hover in one place,
like a hummingbird'

'by their ability'
falcons . Saka .
             of the sun
        that hovers over the page
reading the world.

So one reads the page until the image comes,
moons of Granada
drenched in smooth fountains
while the bird hovers
over the chosen word.

How to read.
How to bare it, how to bear
that those smooth thighs and hips
are sometimes wet from the fountain spray
or drenched with moons
swimming at midnight
               or sometimes dry
               in the choked night,
how to live
a day or a year
picking out what matters.

How to live
under the shadow
of the bird that picks me out

under the carpet.
Sweep the pattern of the carpet under the carpet
where the pattern can sink through
& become the floor.
To walk on the floor then
is to accept the condition of my effort.
I walk on my effort.
To read is to walk

again I said, Arise
& know the water
for the first time,
                    arise, the text
is open.
To wait all that while
to 'find' an image
those amorous tissues of the night
around the fountain,
women, moons, women
& to wait
all that while for an image & not
be able to live,
not live with that memory
pouring forward
where the moon
awakens
            above the cloud-band on the rim of the carpet,

the fountain sloshes over,
                    the sky
              suddenly trapped on the floor.
And put that in a text.
To trap the moon in a carpet.
To unremember.
To trap the moon in a puddle on marble.
To have made the effort,
to walk through the image
to swim in the moon.
To have made the ground
                    & not submitted to it.
To hover over the text.
To read.

Wanderers Nachtlied

The children of the children.
Our hope was low in the earth,
a taste or city name,
a chance to turn
our clothing inside out.

                Eros was my master
         & now I wonder
if I ever had another,
              he who shaped
all these relentless subtle roads.

Magic Annandale

The white pines
The sky
in so dense a place
deepest
memory of the pines
tips almost black against

this road
more than
any other
goes

at any season
twilight
luminous wooden houses long ago painted white

The Confession

I have occupied the smallest space
challenging in my way
even the precise fervor of cats
to compress in sunlight
those immeasurable bodies
which are their own ultimate geography

I have confused this contraction with virtue
and have made silence
into a sort of religion
until I forget what half-heard question
from a young mouth itself half-
trembling with listless shyness
crossed over a day later to my mind
on a grey morning
when there are trucks outside
stopped in front of quiet houses

I have tried to answer with words and not-words
until this confession itself
seems comfortably beside the point
lyrical elaborate and safe

If I was quiet it was only that I was thinking
If I was thinking of something it was you I think
If it was you it's all the stranger I didn't answer when you spoke.

Σνμμαχος εσσο

And I ask for help too, Aphrodite,
fight at my side so I am not in that sad
terrible way lonely as I hurry towards
your holy creatures.

The Queen of Between

Frau Binnen
I woke up thinking,
the Queen
of Between.

Her name
is that great description,
her being
is location.

Be, bee & between,
a melissary
agent of intercourse
coupled

across the octaves
dominants, lurid
brackets,
thighs.

.2.

Women
of within
from dream
I call them

roses
of an inner
springtime
all time

excluded
except their
sense of
when

& then again
nested snug
or nestled
in the air

petals
unfolded
one at no time
then all

.3.

Massive dense
as if the intellect
were shadow
and the shadow soil

and cauliflowers
blossomed
inside this light
to taste

of no time
but there
they are
interior

commissars
of every order
whose summons
is this caress.

Garnets

People who are sure
& who have learned their letters well
as children
when there was nothing to distract them
from the fall of sunlight through big windows
splayed out on the floor
where the clean floorboards were
suddenly ornate with dust

lean on me now, let me
push towards a clarity
easy for them hard for me
because most of my letters
are still in the walls of my mind
like garnets in rock

the sort I once stood for an hour
prying out of a schist block
on a stone bridge up the west side
with a blue penknife I'd won years before
playing Fascination at Rockaway

red, deep violet,
blood but not arterial,
dark but not secret,
                        garnets
sensual, color of lust remembered
but not prospect,
                    no vista
            of American Women
huger than history
                coming towards the poem

their arms wrapped in silver studded with
dark
    small color
that remembers instead a single evening
built out elaborately, rehearsedly,
around a complex series of touches
I believed in more than the sun
and for whose sake, touch,
I have neglected
my letters and my sums
                    to know nothing
      but the intricate want.

Lust is not the name of it.
Lust is forthright hungry obvious,
satisfiable. This is not.
It appropriates what it knows
into an unconsenting analysis,

it solves the bright skin
inward towards the infolded touchstone,
sign
    of its only accuracy.

≡

I would like to find a thing I can talk about
long enough to reach from here to there
here being the start of a piece of sulphite paper
white as Mallarmé
and there being a full-found n-dimensional being
whose name is You
and whom I have both found and foretold
while other orders of arrogance
kept me arriving at your shrine

at your shine I should say
the gleam of original light
donated to my darkness as your first message
maybe your last
your form Your
Form
towards which this haste to discover or be in or be

the thing I have not yet succeeded in imagining
would be a barebone connective unresisting
glassy with honesty
it would pasture us all the green season
and let us lie in warm byres come the winter
the equation is elusive

the habits of my culture and my acculturated body
suggest plausibly this connective I'm looking for
is a part of this same my body encouraged
to go burrow in a part of yours or in yours
and that in fact is itself isnt it time after time
a miracle of habitation
of pouring of touching of falling asleep and waking

and where are we then
are we then

somewhere on the other side of identity
where there is a population
I need to reach and blend with as you are
to become
any of the wonderful destinations of the heart
so this fact of love does not stay just a fact on paper
sensitive and shameless as a thermometer
recording the ups and downs of never getting there at all.

Ship Burial

I am your beloved
as it happens

a great fish
it is or I am

out of the geometric deeps
off Cape This

forever.
There is no chance.

*

The ship turned down,
                    the Viking
burial

    it is not a church it is not a ship
though it has the waist of a ship
& the turn
                    around the forehead peak
to a fogged-in north
the Hel road

                    it is the Sign
in which they come to die,
                              vesica piscis, & to turn
with any Luck

to woman again,
to turn

32

woman again to
my needs I am turned.

I am your beloved
hulldown in sour earth

where your honey fell.

*

What they are buried in is not a ship
or if a ship
            then such a deep vessel
as reaches almost up past Cassiopeia
seated on her soft complex throne unto
her heart, or the heart,

                        what they are buried in
is her sign

womb
to come again

& the rocks that rim
this circumstance

in our northern fact
teeth him to earth

to come again
by this great

Door at last.

I am your

beloved who wields this sign.

≡

I wish I could hold on to what the boy held onto
        when he jumped from the dock into the
        dark glass of the East River
that fine cold used water coming up around
        to cup his cock & probe him & stick close
        the way water does
always right there, always in contact
& never letting a thing much less a thought
        come between it & the fulfillment of its own nature
to touch & touch equally,
to die if it has to right there on the skin.

The Beatrice

I was allowed to be serious
the song she sang
was like a puzzle,
it hassled me

for the sake of some recollection:
Where was the sea?
Would she bring it to me?
Was there a way

for us to be together?
Would she remember? Did I
in fact remember? Was there
a fact to be remembered?

Was there a sea?
These were the overtones
of her terrestrial symphony,
her noise, sigh of her body

walking by & the air
quick around her waist
to have knowledge of her
central twist

that made her body
such a song, complex, wrong,
a mistake for me to hear,
I stuffed

my blood into my ears
so I would not overhear
the long exposition
of her first theme:

This me of me, this rapture
I project as my body
(she said) is your necessity.
You can know nothing

all your life except me.
I am who does you good
beyond your reach
but sometimes tired let you

touch me come touch me.

The Mediatrix

It's what the tip of the tongue does
alone in the sun

what I heard I hear:
blank birds welcoming spring in.

What happens is that desire is perfected. The wild need to have becomes the
wild need to know. "Let me see it," we said as children, meaning Put it in
my hands, let me touch it. O put it in my hands. Hand it to my hands.
Touch was the great mediator. Mediatrix, was the classroom word we
learned, Mary was, of all graces, Woman mediator of all graces of all grace.
Let me see it. Let the grace of the situation touch me.

The tip of the sun's tongue
lights this day to music.
Early. As if I had died in the night & been
brought back as the harsh shadows
of the hill, of the ash trees under the hill
stretching down towards a car wet with what
sun does to frost.

As the shadow returning stretches
toward my eyes.
Everything I ever was
spoke to you then.
                    The earth
returns. That it is ethical,
            a hotbed of situations
in which we are resolved.

38

2.

From the nun's soft face
harsh shadows, chalk clean woman
smell, the word raptly uttered, Mary
mediatrix of,
                use me it said, use me don't
touch me she
seemed to say,
Mediate all
grace I'll let you see.
It was as if a promise,
it was a promise

that seeing
would be holding,
a mind would touch.

Vast lazy windows of spring classroom.
School is some trick women thought up,
to come & go & make me return
morning after morning. The instruction.

But it is this way, always, was:
To see & think 'hold.' To hold & think 'have.'
And never know, never know.

It is their behavior, your behavior
I loved, how you do, how do you
do, good morning we said, time's a
wasting,
                time's a waking, love is
waiting.

           I think
to be casual about it, to have fallen
for your trick again you don't even
intend.
           It is natural
alas in the mode of light.

Sometimes I think you can't help doing it
& then I have nowhere to hide.

≡

My lap is
Lazarus
coaxed from sleep,
that long white marble vacancy
smelled bad
    I woke
at a loving preposterous voice
calling
not my name
but her own
on which I rose.

The Ceiba Tree of the Tzotzil

is like Yggdrasil.
It goes up through all worlds
& features this.
We are necessary
to its immense design.
We are like leaves or like feathers.
There are even birds.
We must not have airs
or large designs.
It behooves us
to climb.
We do what we can.
From time to time
someone or something
fucks us
as it can.
This may be a pleasure
or a meek obstacular
furrow in the smooth.
Fourier: unrequited love
is the lowest
step on the ladder of Love.
But start there,
vita nuova, so on,
on up, up to go,
go with you, radiant
lady whose shadow
is the fact or trunk of this tree.
The next step up
he says is monogamy.

To one & from one.
Utterly perceived
& then to go.
Mahogany. All the different
woods is knowing you.
In your stages
of our progress
getting to know
till later this single
kiss distributes
itself through all the
leaves & then.

The Long March

My father made me begin thinking in the body of my mother
on Christmas night 1934
when the First Route Army
was between Pienchai and Wengkulung.

While the army crossed mountains and rivers and deserts
and rivers again and rivers and rivers
for eight thousand miles
my mother carried me patiently

answering every question of my nature
as it searched inside her
for the tools and weapons and strategies it would need.

Even after the terrible empty grassland in the north
wadded under grey clouds went on forever
she went on

till in the heat of September
in the border regions between Kansu and Shensi
after nine months she lay down
and for three days writhed
to say me most exactly into the world,
to suffer in her body this sign of being accurate

and I came into the breath
while the exhausted heroes of the great deliverance
trudged the eleven conscious miles between Luching and Hsin-ssu.

The Menelaus

Be sure to hold the least of it in your cool arms
how do they stay so in this intolerable climate
as if the fever-snake had bitten the whole earth
& the river bleeds.
                              I have come for you at last.
You are my possession: or for the sense of you
as my possession it has been fought. Whatever was
now has been burnt down, died down. I came here
in my own shape but lost it on the way.
                                        Your name
is what I chiefly remembered. Sometimes the spread
of your legs as you leaned back to receive me.
But mostly an image, if an image, of you coming
up out of a sun-infested pool. I dreamt it once,
never saw it so, for all the pools of our kinder
kingdom. Queendom. It was not a place without you.

≡

May snow up Mead Mountain,
down here a white an old
white horse looks
out of a red barn
onto the earth,
the earth.

Parthenon

for C.R.

It was tired enough for me to look at the picture
snapshot of the Parthenon white not honeyed stone
under bluest sky.
                    As I watched I wondered
will I cry? Will there be a poem called then
"Weeping over the Parthenon" as if I were a god of that
terrible hour, weeping over an image?
Why would I cry? I felt the deliberate tear ducts
ponder the question with me, a preliminary
discourse of my fluids, tears are lymph are sperm
is vision. Who do I want & won't admit it?
Who do I see without seeing, my whole body
dissolving inward to the calm of water? Who is this sun?
I felt the tender pressure's increment—
would I cry? Would the rhetoric drown me & the City?
Could I identify the grief that opened the picture so?
The columns are impossible to count. Eight
along the front, why eight? I wanted them odd.
The columns on the side are imponderable, lost
in shadow & perspective—like all numbers, most
precious of our thoughts, dissolving, onward, gone.
I wanted an odd number to bear witness
to the disorder in my breast, heart-cave
from which a spirit comes out not often
into this fierce daytime. I feel the heat I watch.
I am of those who turned away from sunlight,
Cro-Magnon is it, hid in the caves, polarized light
of clouds & rain & sensual moonlight, to see my true love
in the true light of unburning clearness. Athens?
I am so far from this place.

I would hate
the baking cloudless sky, the money-bright
tourist atmosphere, noisy city of opinions below.
Doxa. This curious memory of an exalted order
all my life eluded me. Reproaches me, makes
tears get ready but they don't flow.
Parthenon. Building of the Virgin mind
set out in space, integral, self-involved.
Not bored by even numbers, as I am. Eternal rage
uncorks in me to wreck this place
more than time & Turks & scholarship have ruined it.
This structure is reproach. Renew the sources of your life
it tells me, as an earlier embassy told Rilke: *Change*.
Renew the sources. Bathe in a simpler water. Cry.

The woman takes the picture from my hand
after a long time. "Here," she says, "this block of stone.
It seems to have a shadow on it. It has a face
worn almost smooth, a young man's face
carved in the fallen stone
looks from the mind and smiles." Cry.
Whose face laughs disguised as shadow?
This snapshot of the virgin world's unfallen uprights
drags at my tears. I am afraid I will be alone
someday, jammed in my body under a hot sky.
I am afraid of the sky. What capitulations
have I signed to live in the hook of the world?
Why does it hurt me to look at this?
Because my own face, whose else could it be, looks
out at me from the rock and says "Your desire is the only order."

A Woman from Connaught

My great-great-great-great-grandmother
on my father's father's father's mother's side
I remember with the curious vividness of all creatures.
She was small
and her perfectly round eyes had not yet
been lost in the big green slit-eyes lewdness of the Kelly eyes.
She travelled once in her long life down
from the north and west where her fathers
had been kings, and their wives and mothers
innocent harlots of sunshine,
paid by green life for all their travail,
wild sex of white-thighed women till she came along.

The exploits stopped then.
A long smouldering
match had reached at last her philosophic powder.
She exploded into a restless stillness,
read books in four languages, wore her round
eyes milky with cataract but still,
even at the last of things, thought she could see
the devoted moon go up
over the rafters of her slatternly house,
all dim spiders and dirt floors she guessed.
But the floors were good oak parquet
and her own bees made the wax that gleamed
high over her mind in the white rooms.

Their echo I still hear, rooms or bees,
song of their summing
all the names and numbers of the flowers
that writhed unseen in her garden. She was not sexy.
She thought things into place and held them there.
She could hardly tell if the candles were lit.

The skirts of her redingote trailed
at times across her feet. She thought them rats
and marvelled at their boldness,
wondered should she not be firmer with the servants,
if indeed those english-speaking shadows
were her servants, not mere ghosts
of all her enemies come back to mock
with unclear whispers at the edge of rooms.

The fields are always blank, she thought,
and autumn rebukes the summer's brashness.
It is empty. They are empty.
So blank there had to be a force somewhere
austere and honest. She called it God
and thought men ought to honor it
by books in many languages, and keeping still,
and sitting in large rooms alone.
                                        Oh God
she prayed, keep the smell of the stables away.
Dont let me hear the wasps yawning all spring long.
Dont let me hear the children singing
or Sarah's petticoat slither on wet grass.
Let me know you in an Irish silence,
sweet dumb of heart & clever-mouth & loving.
Let there be nothing but love and then not even that.

But when the gardener mowed the lawns
the smell of the grass came
in the long windows and stood in the room like kings.
From her I have my love of cloudy days,
long pauses in the conversation, silences
at the ends of lines of poetry, thick symphonies,
quiet women and their heavy gods.

The Siren

Of what can we be sure
in what secure?
those choruses,
                  their clamor.
Dawn ridge over
not where I traveled
but to the mind-meant labyrinths
of beast desire
to be more so.
                        He does not tell us
             she was beautiful.
That typecasting of Eros
he suspends.
            Lifts up
that vernicle & then we cry,
marred by her evil smell.
It is the same woman seen again
with lust, & then with lust lifted away—
it costs a kingdom to see her pure again.

*

It is not to be beastly to touch her
though the *want to* is doggy,
degrades the wanter who could so light
reach out his thinking to be with her.
Bad dog. To want to
           & not do.
So that the want
becomes a template
that denies her,
hides her.

51

The bad dog peers through,
howls at her pale moon.

Lontano

Late: Could there ever
be a city that forgives
all our bodies
into warm rooms, broad

terraces from the clouds
on down to the bartered lights
I wait also in the windows
an iron bird

or just his beak is,
tearing at the sky
so far away that here
only the soft of it falls?

Dance Suite Sung on a Phrase of D. H. Lawrence

The dance grew more subtle & the same
time more
explicit as their bodies turned, a round
of slender bodies lifted
subtly off the dance floor by
musical aggression or

the dance more subtle, their hips
hardly handled by
                        their partners turned
explicit as the music faltered,
there were candles
swung down from the ceiling on
the same old wagon wheel upended

& outside on Tinker Street
there was no snow, but over,
over all of the, dance, was snow
mid-May Mead Mountain

swung from the sky a light she
danced among them, they
were they & only
                        danced, the same
old wheel around the still

dark dance hall of an old enclosure
moved with lights more subtle
as the dancers touched each
other only by the floor they landed on.

2.

O explicit light
that makes the world so subtle
I came to this town before

for the dance here made explicit
of how the dancers, chosen by chance
it seemed were really subtle sisters

subtle brothers we have always lived together
I knew her here before the flesh & for

one long weekend, was it, came then
so I could see the old man.
But how could I look

at any man
away from where she danced?
Was dancing

the old wheel
hung down from heaven for the slowest tread

of the old man of the old man
swung among the girls who drifted
kindly to his time

dreamy, curving
May snow on his mountain.

3.

But I couldnt bear to spend the night
among these mountains,
wouldnt sleep out of the city
out of the fear of the dance
that might seize me, carry
from the subtle of desire to the explicit need

till I was rooted in this world then
for the sake of a dumb dance,
this fleshy move that comes to her so easy.

4.

I think what I wanted was their bodies
as a silent landscape for my travels.

I didnt know a day would come
I would want the mountain to answer me.

5.

Men talk more than any women do
& would spend their lives if they could
slowly turning phrases in their mouths
beneath the looped glow-wax of
the wagon wheel of dwindling lights.

The candles make shadows & the shadows dance:
nobody knows more than that.

6.

They changed their partners.
The sun went up.
Late afternoon the snow was
still up there, shielded,

& in the soft cwm
seen from the golf-course
sheltered there too.
Sleeping with people

how wonderful that is,
four-quarter time or common measure,
each with each, our warm legs
rescued from the dance, entwined.

7.

Sleeping with subtle people.
To be explicit
I want to sleep with you
I want our dance to be

dance spread out over the whole world
where people make explicit all their subtle labors
praising & being praised.

People with people
working the world.
                    The world is work
sleeping subtly

among the explicit dance
that goes inside to grow
                              side to side by side.
Sleeping with people more subtle
than any dance,
the candle burns down
till the last light of it
is the first of dawn

& bodies naturally tired
sleep with each other
part in part,
the smell of the dance still on them.

In the furrows & the wallowed bed
the dance grows more explicit
until by light
day subtler than sleep succeeds.

Women of the Bois de Boulogne

In the Bois de Boulogne shows a shiny car.
Its back door is open.
Two naked women
are getting in, their backs are towards us.
They look politely at each other
offering precedence. A formal
sapphic pastourelle
such as men desire
                    to see.
                            Their hair
is fifty years ago.

*

Is there a chauffeur to drive them where?

I volunteer.
How shiny the car is,
were they always so clean?

The leaves.

The shadows
the light
leaves.

*

How their bodies are brighter than polished chrome.
How they give more light than they get.
How we glow in the dark & no one knows it.

*

But the secret lover
sees.

*

How snug it will be inside.
The warm plush upholstery plum or fawn,

their legs arranging, their eyes
distracted by the passing trees.

*

Where does the car go
that takes my imagination so far from this place
this river & leaf shade
to that place in the Bois?
What does it run on, super, superfina,
octane of the blood or brain
to power it?
         No,
it is drawn
as the wind draws,

chariot of lovers, chariot of the Rose.

Tyranny of imagined women!

*

The picture was taken in 1925.
I didnt get to Paris till '54.
These women
no longer looked the same.
They had oatmeal of the thighs.
They thought more about money.
They did not live in the districts I visited.
I passed them in the Place Maubert
& didnt know them.
They did not remember the picture
or where the car travelled
if they ever really climbed inside it,
did not forever step
up on the running board
into the warm dark that doesnt go anywhere—
that's how they thought of sex.
They had poor memories.
They had gained some weight.
They had rosaries.

*

So the real world, so-called,
would make a curse of the imagination.
It would say: because the beautiful limbs
are withered or graceless now
& no one yearns to stroke them
or probe their generous bodies,
these women are sad ironic memories
& the car is junk
melted down & the trees
even the trees are thick-waisted
& the carved initials too high to read.

But the real world, as ever, lies.
The car still goes. The maidens,
unchanged, can be followed
into the invisible city of Fotografie
where images arise in the red dark
to be worshipped by us
                        slaves of our eyes.

*

This is all about the
left buttock of the right woman
whose straight-nosed face looks lewd & candid
over at her nervous partner, her shy
lover for the sake of the picture.
These women
are showing us their asses.
That is,
they are showing us
what they themselves cannot see.
That is the meaning of the picture.
That is what art is about:
Latin *ars*, "art or craft or skill,"
skill to show
English *arse*, flattened by Boston to American *ass*.

Art is to show other people
what you cant see yourself.

*

I suppose them in their moving car
through the cities of northern France,
sometimes waving from windows,
sometimes making love in market towns
while quiet peasants watch through tinted glass
with reverence they learned in the stables—
did they tint glass in '25?

Sometimes, just as they are,
they get out of the car
& climb the dank cochlear stairways of cathedrals,
fingers of their free hands
trailing lightly over worn stone roundels
carved with alchemical images.

On top of the tower, Laon maybe,
they peer off towards Belgium or Broceliande,
then come back to their saloon-car
whose engine did not stop purring while they clomb.

The girl on the left remembers
the Rebis, the hermaphrodite
shy as she.
                The girl on the right
remembers the carving of a lizard
mouth open screaming inside some fire.

*

Does this touch last forever
of hand on skin on eye?

Does the thing seen once seen
have no other life than the mind

& the mind no other life but it & all
like it that unveiled before?

*

I dream all night of the way they behave.
I see them turn & embrace each other
so fully that I too am embraced, I share
the dusty comfort of the silent car,
I who am in them & of them, being in the world;
I dream of their behavior and call it *body*.

The ineptness of my name does not make them falter.
The name of her (you know who)
I also inscribe here, it is :
Everyone is for the sake of everybody else.
We belong to those who see us & use us,
belong to the eye & the touch.

*

And the shy one, the one whose face
is only nose-tip, cheekbone, sense
of a reserved brunettish calm,
says: You cant see me. I belong to your mind.

———

The poem thanks Nathaniel Tarn, who sent from Paris the postcard that bears the image.

Shiva

what does the bee think
when her flower
writhes in the wind
she struggles to stay in

*

I was Shiva.
I sat on a mountain
top was cold my
sufferings had been predicted.
My mother warned me

of everything.
I was huge in my austerity.
Now they worship me by walking naked
ashes in their eyes

touching no one.
I touched everything
& was called god.

Surplus-labor
enlarged my altar
until I was owner
of every grief

& wind brought fires closer:
sleek of their bodies
those dakinis I lifted
on me & I over them
my left arms holding their
hips them in to me

until I was syntactic confusion
& shivered
with everything pressing into my skin too
I was no less pierced than the world I
shoved my way in

*

they worship me as ice they find me
as ice when I last as
fire when they find me

The Traveler

the interruptions are a sort of ride

Bitter cabbage of the moon
left to rot in a songless night

or to die of confusion
alone like Lorca

under the animal trees?
Nowhere to go
but the original country of all

I follow the tracks of fieldmice to it
past the dead raccoon & the cherry tree

dead before blossoming.

The Balustrade

When I was a child in flannel pajamas
going down from my room with my left hand on the rail
I called it bannister.
I was frightened then of black leopards coming

noiselessly up & nosing the door open.
Or being dead, hung by the neck yet swinging
into view as the closet door swings open,
hanging against the painted wood like neckties.

Baby blue. Years later I came to know
the untrustworthiness of fear & desire.
The rail is marble, mounted on small urns,
& along it trail the listless faint rosy fingers

of many young women in white or silk.
They look off at the sea
behind me as far as they are before me.
I look up & admire them with my whole life

& hope to catch a glimpse of white thighs
in the shadowy gaps between the ornate urns.
It does not happen so. In the ultimate shadow
the panther prowls in the formal garden.

Sometimes I find the rose-trees savaged,
flower head beaten down as if by rain.
When there is no rain ever & the sea dew alone
makes the grass grow. I see her pawprints

on the unglazed tiles of the walkways
between the knot-twists of the herb garden.
She browses on tarragon & mint.
I call it balustrade for the formality,

for the white, for their well-turned legs
idly moving them out of reach & almost
out of eyeshot along the front of the palazzo.
I grip the rail & try not to turn on the light.

Ode on the Two Hundredth Birthday of This Commonwealth

Divine agriculture of festivals
grown up from the tilth of common time
dunged with all our nightfalls—
o und die Nächte
those little superscript letters
that darken or lighten the pitches of things, colors, hands
reach out to make sure you're still there.

Still here. Skirts. Roba. Cloth specifies.
The anthem is epistemological,
wanted to know if "the flag is still there,"
Does the percept last in the mind?
As a child I knelt before her image
pretending I was tying my shoe—
see, there is a use for shoelaces,
el stations, children, posters, knees.
I prayed with my whole body
Give me into her, give her to me.

I worshipped the sexual as such,
the women who would & who do,
gleam of their liberties, starlight
flesh of their permissions. Not purity.
What exalted was the intensity
with which they entered the sexual world
& drew me ever after. Pornolatry,
this Tyrian ardor. These confessions
always remind me of a city, I think
New York, but the women & the weather
are consistently, but not continuously,
wrong. Which is the city where those images

70

come best together? Coming together.
Twins marry twins in Iowa City,
the left-handed ones are older—the left is older.
"Interior is anterior" said Barfield's mentor,
"You've been listening to Bartok," the girl said;
she played Bartok, the ring or circle
closes on the adept's hand. Microcosm.

Bookstore in Sacramento. Figtree
out the back window in Sherman Oaks.
Oranges on windowsills. Deliver me
into this gentle planet, the love
where it is love & the Dove where it is fire.
I kneel at her image whose poster
peels off the wall, beneath it tigers
from all our circuses, Happy Birthday
Beast America, her legs appear again
fifteen strata down. This was Troy
behind the trees, on the shady spot,
acers, sumacs, basswoods—America

America you need knights (o, und die
Knechte, your servants!), grail-globular America
you need servants, templars in linen
smeared with her blood in the sign of the
America you need Knights to find you & carry you home
your legs wild with desire, up the stairs to
that undefined somewhere it All is about & you know it,
wipe that smile off your face & be worshipped,
America you need me to articulate your praises,
America my blame. A country needs her praises.
You ruin me with the multiplicity of your caress.

Ring on my hand. Bartok came here,
Perse, Schönberg, Kantorowicz, Mann,
Broch on Washington Place rescued
young Charles Olson & his wife—stayed with them,
money & talking. They came
to rescue us, they were our knights
& we their bare-boobed Andromeda on the rocks
patient in our empty-headed unrelatedness.
They rescue us with discourse.

But we came too, even before them, India
we called it & we married them,
gnawed their land away, they want it back
but they are not they, they are us too, copper
like our cheapest coins, beautiful, noisy,
out of place. They are immigrants from time
& falter into our drunken customs, our trucks

grunting by on the bison road now, coyotes
come back, beast fang down to Albany last winter,
they came. America I have always loved you.
What do you care. Who are you to care?
You don't even have ears to hear me
& all those Albanian civil servants
don't have ears "and their legs are wood"
& all the true Zukofskys lead us home.
Louis! You are most America,
prophet only of the next vowel-sound,
prince of phonemes. Now how abashed
I pay him honor, septuagintine Byzantine,
artifex, born in the lifetime of Lenin, *av*.

But so arriving at his text I must confess
life is real when sex is. I am a zealot
of that most common most mysterious religion
& patrol the temple-boundaries all night long for years,
the city, the street defining no other ritual
except to find her there.

Great blue of the sky, of trees, of blue-green cars
I always have, to ride in her body.
To salt copper with the fangs of my love,
that is my knowledge. Dog bark. Fire
cracker breaks, the rockets glare down on us
insufficiently red. But I see green after "as ever,"
no-see-ems bite, summerskin.
The war comes soon. The bomb's early light
where her beauty full of intelligence starts
up over the hell of images & takes all the confusion
of this worship & turns it to a clean simple thing
perhaps her self, a body can be with me

full of silence as I come
close to the sacred birthday of Thunderland.
America the Silver. America the Sky.

El Desdichado

Mockery of birds, missed lines, slipped
dates in calendars, calendulas, rain

salt bodied citizens, the dimpled small
of pink backs, bowling balls, we bend

to lift, he uses his body as a crane
as a machine to carry heavy opacities.

He carries furniture upstairs & doesnt
answer the phone. Heart attack

on every step, & Ungaretti cold Xmas
watches smoke caprioling from the hearth

seeking its own vacancy. Tenth house Mercury.
"Mt Taishan over Pisa." Woman-hill,

Mount Wife. *Zhena moia*, says he,
about his Russia, *my wife*. Irby

keeps quoting that to me till my heart breaks
That a man could feel so, that I feel so

about a land, & lose her, not just a shape
as girls of twenty become matronly, hips spread one day,

I kiss her ass anyhow, the birds are intricate,
today is intricate, time is assembling

|

74

all its destinations & velocities, he sets
the oak thing down on the highest step.

Master Dante, Messer Arnautz, I am here at last,
come do me honor—I also ate distances,

I also, Uranus in 4°, was an exile
before her face, that bitter one with such sweet flanks

turned from me. I take comfort from her worshippers
destroyed before me with long years. With trees.

With olives & high schools & sad roadhouses
grunting at midnight, hearth, old words, home,

the breaking point & no break. No catastrophe.
All alive under the incessant lilacs, alone.

Quarante

'O moon of my delight'
that knows
a self beyond
phenomena
a wheel or breakfast
turned
—broken—
from all the easts
is red
the laborers
sweat at the
grunt under her eight
pairs of tires

the bridge passes.
O moon of my
undoing was it
the swift snarl
of the astrologer
doubting all things
aligned,
or not aligned,
beckoning
catastrophe down
into the field
of what we think
is happening,

divided land.
The Civil War
instead of ending

polarized itself
down the sagittal suture—
this polarity
turn after turn
divided & starred off
arms to infinity—
we
were the spores of a new
galaxy grown,
grown out of our minds

& madness
became the sanity
of the universe.
We realm.

America
is a story
without heroines.
All the names
we are taught to remember
do not mean her
where she arose
& lay about her
here on this
what kind of shore?

attractive
like her mouth
a little open
tempting to dream

but some liberties
it turned out
were unforgivable
we slept
from each other
away

now if I would carry
all my hopefulness
back into my body
or field of direct
sensation
would that not be death?
I ast her

& no answer—
in the heart
of the crown jewels
the king found
his rarest emerald
the Stone of
Doubt
      for whose sake
death sent its children
into the world,

why emerald?
in the enigmatic glance
of Venus
as she is fucking,
all loss & all undoing
can be read—

as well as love & prospering.
Ambiguous.
The starchart
goes up in flames.

It is a damp season
in a damp house.
Mildew
that ancient word
is silent, brusque
airsnake to poison
suddenly a book
—drips with venom—
not unusual
taste
of the library
smell of the damp.
I coil down in.
To read
is to fail her
safe.
To write
is persiflage
exalted incense
plumes the altar
reeks. But what
she wants is death
of will
at least.
And Will himself
boiled
to ease her fever.

How she outs.
How she unks
the fork ball raider
to blunt
against any wail,
cup of his whines
poured out
infantine grief
below some ground—
cant they hear
the groans from those caves,
grown men yowling
at her indifferent carriage
who had been elegant
in self-exposition
to them early,
sleek of her intentions
blazed into sight?

Membering by pieces.
Archeology
of any loving night—
as if redemption
lay in the analysis—
does it,
lay analysis, what it
brings to mind?
Redemption
is what is brought to mind
of all the loving
nights went down
to snuff under Hissarlik

the news of her come?
Sleek of her thigh
graced with mingled
are they waters & whose?
And hers?
From her window
of all our houses
alone
Pluto may be seen
spurting across the sky.
But the surds
those silences
between the numbers when
the old brick wall
jagged top with
broken bottles of
the home for girls
up for reform against
was it Ralph avenue who
no a place in Paris
silences
between the numbers
sometimes a *pi*
comes to illuminate

le Roi de Bicêtre
King of Bedlam I
with salve of bdellium
kohl'ed my eyelids
into a mask
I thought was woman
& turned my transsexual

glance
        inside
to see if I could find one
there
        in the middle

in the middle
of the beauty.
So it was a home
for Bad Girls they
told me frightened me so
evilly the clang
of traffic passing
the sinister
(inside the body) quiet
of that cursed place
behind the walls

even the broken glass was old
its shards
glinted in no sunlight
was badness
disobedience?
was it bad
to disobey the Sun
masked as my father
my mother
what did I find
inside, sinister
silence inside the body
except the belch or fart
forbidden noise

was spoken from,
& if that's what it *said*
what would it be thinking
all the while
it is Paris
the raw red madhouses
of some working quarter
where the hooting lunatics
analyse hour by hour
the decomposition of the moon
into its component sulphurs
& proclaim, their feet
jammed down into the bleeding glass,
their awful transneptunian
chemistry new found
from the top of the wall
before the dogs drag them down
are there dogs?

there are dogs, they
licked the blood & scum of burn
off Strindberg's hands
in this same city only
fifty years before or sixty
or the dragon bent
a bow arched opisthotonos
over the toits de Paris
the blisters the blisters
gushing pus & heavy water
into the gutter I watched
along Atlantic Avenue
only thirty years after that before

where the girls
had sat being evil
baring their scanty secrets to

hide them hide them
behind the baked brick
sleazy in Brooklyn rain
projected into the dank maisons-dieu
of Paris, grunt
of alchemists
their scorched lungs
their last philosophy,

sulphur! secret
universe of terror
clenched in the common world!
sulphur the cat
stalking with quicksilver eyes
the numinous quarry
even I could see
beneath their dark behavior
their shadows
on the wet ailanthus trees
on both sides of the wall

I do not know woman
know women
I do not understand—
the mask I looked with
was the only face I saw
or I saw nothing
till I looked

over the wall
in the lumens of orgasm saw
one like myself
far off advancing
his mind on horizons
& headed there
myself,
I was this self
reaching out
I thought but there
I had gone beyond the wall
still locked
imagination in
while the holistic one
—imageless, holy, silence—
ran quickly on
sure as a panther to pursue
the quick of the world

& find her here
turned there
into another order
of being
I had to drop
free of my hold
to encounter

specifically:
had to drop red
Brooklyn brick alchemy
the girl in the gutter
punished

by the wall of appearances
beyond which
nothing
if I could not

not scale the wall
abandon the wall,
it falls
inward only
it is the fall
of transmutation
to be crushed by
what comes down

even if the cloud
& the brick fall
& I fell
tangled with ivy
in the ruin
of

& only that way
annihilate the clutched
obsessions
o bitter bloods
of archeologies
to find those actual nights
& analyze
them into their loves
& failures

is that not chemistry again

I failed the first time
sulphur into sense

the barrier?

From which always out

the ring
broken
of organic form

II

Miles under water.
The devil
comes out of a hole
in what we think
at that moment
the ground.
What we think is the ground.
The devil
comes
out of a hole in
what we think.
The devil comes out of
a hole in language.
It is for instance
birch trees. It is
limes. There is a sky,
house over lindens.

The lover needs more sleep this
needs more sleep.

O love all I can give you
is a dream, I mean what I dream
I mean, I mean it
when I dream. The flag?
The long lents
took the meat away.
Can I? Learn to talk.
The flag
is simpler, flames
over the house.

The men try to build a school.
Let us laugh at them.
What should a school
smell like they ask.
Can a school
kill the devil?
Can it liberate
the good of us from hell.
Can it break hell.
O these flaming
intentions of our laughter these
men trying to break hell.

A school?
A school would be to take
the devil & wash him in language
wash his wordless gawping
mouth out with language—
baptize him
in the name of Name.

Soon the little boy
will go to school.
The men, Colet & More & Dewey
have built the school
& broken it in pieces
& shaken the pieces
out all over the world

this guesswork
like the sounding shell
behind the alabaster pulpit
these good men stand in
sweating with ideals
they shiver down on

this little boy.
Their flaming brains
set fire to Quarante

who is in the backyard
digging his little trenches
across the garden
between the flagging
under ivy & the
hydrangea
& in the furrows sets
all his manhood
to play at war—
at that period
his virility was lead soldiers
mostly from England.
The war was still new.

Quarante would measure his love
ever after by
how many lead soldiers he would sacrifice

(before he caved the glacis in
& filled the trench up
—his father scolded—
entombing all his men
in some strange Egypt.
Never come again.
His friends were stealing his soldiers
piece by piece his father also said.

WHERE ARE MY SOLDIERS?

These powers
rested against my thighs—
it was the elements
made me rouse,
Nora in water, Paul on earth

—& years later,
when they were gone from the house
his father would wonder
about other little boys
digging in the garden,
finding all those soldiers
from a war they never heard of

(the colors I mean
come from the words

& there is skill,
a musical
chopping, pausing,
whence an order
of beauty arises,

dead men in the ground,
no theory

(but the ink is grey
& the long afternoon becomes a quick night
full of strife

if the words
could remember themselves

not just helpful
etymology
but the nuclear physics of,

particles of *this* word

(the word
manifest

more lightning
than analysis.

The Mix

the thought
of being here
I am a devil
sometimes

& I make
trouble
I admit it
It is my

kind of flower.

I

It is eight o'clock
The large man gives the small man
a boat in bed

The small hand reaches up
the large hand holds
The boat is big
almost as the bed

A woman watches
& there is a window

The time is locked in the clock
A floor is not regular
The boat has a flag
a funnel & a flag

Why would he want a boat in bed?
Fezzes on their heads
A moon is wrapped in the flag.

SCHOLIA

Ia

I bet the austere reader seven piasters
that I know where the boat is going & he does too.

It is travelling north past the Imperial City
(which used to be called K-polis in its heyday)

& will soon wallow into the hyacinthine waters
of the Inland Ocean. O rare girl with blue eyes

shadowed from Cimmerian clouds! Crimean that is,
the plains of Asia that threaten to swallow the boat.

But it veers east, toward Trabzon. It is beautiful
as clouds. It is full of birds.

Ib

The small man is a child
we can be certain from the lack
of face hair on his face

And from the fact of giving.
Only a child is given things,
Only a child could use a boat in bed

II.

It is seven o'clock
after or before
There is no evidence it's the next morning
Maybe the boat is dead

The man lives

It is another house
where the clock is smaller
Venesection they call it
where the blood is let

The surgeon cuts blood from the upper arm
right arm
The patient's
eyes are open   His wife gasps
at the gush of blood

the child like a little tiny man
looks sick to his stomach   Daddy

The blood arcs in
three streams to a basin
like a chamber pot or some hard vegetable
The blood is just blood

it must be a joke book,
the blood.

III.

He looks through his roof
at what are they trees

I took them for haughty spirits of flame
there is no evidence for such love
standing up above the houses
stiff & teaching us to burn

No
It is snow
snow on the roof of the next house
& tracks run up it

He sees the tracks

He is in a hole in his own roof

Through a hole in his top
he sees tracks leading up

leading down
spirits of flame
are cypresses with snow on them
rare snow

Rare snow of eastern parts where men are brown
& look with great noses through the roof of their house

There is no clock & it is dark

Maybe he came up through the roof
to tell the time

to judge by stars but there are no stars

tracks in the snow

his eyes
move along them

to where there is no time either.

SCHOLION III

Who made the tracks was it a thief

what kind of thief has such small feet

was it a child or a thief dressed up as a child
furnished by fences with child-sized feet

was it a beast

By one mode of counting there are 32
individual prick-holes in the snow
each made by a foot
say
or by a stick
if a thief with no feet ran up with two sticks

parallel lines?

If thirty two, then Qabbalah.

If thirty two
then the man in the roof is a qabbalist
& there was no thief
& the house below him is full of books

Mice eat his feet
while he watches the cold moon
& snow slither down the cypress branches not
meant to hold snow

If there was no thief
then the holes are the counts of the ways of the
thoughts in the head of the man who was no thief
who put the house there & the man in the house
& the artist to draw it & me to write it down
& who pardons this confusion though He doesnt like it

And if that's how it is
then there is nothing that exists
except snow on a roof with
tracks leading somewhere
made by something now gone

Or the roof made its own tracks
eyes to see with
made its own hole & the man
to look through the hole & admire the tracks

you beautiful holes.

The Court Painter

How can I show you the truth of
anyone without his face you ask?
The face is the last thing I paint,
& the least important.
It is there to trick the subject
into thinking he is one,
that he has been 'represented.'
But where *he* is is in a fold
of cape, shadow of a label,
wrinkle between elbow & those wide
gold stripes that tell how great he is.

For days sometimes I leave them,
portraits perfect all but the faces.
Each time I wait until some woman
(I am never hired to paint women)
moves in the murk of the paint
& tells me the painting of this thick
field marshal or commissar is done.
Then I quickly hang the face on,
right where they'll see it & stop looking.

Should Eros have

& then the come of it
(the whole world out there not the mingiest flyer
soaring Mitsubishis of nostalgia down
into the craven lagoons of our protection

leach-field,
                        to dehydrate the shit
& shift the water into our time-transformer,
big ion-column Earth,
                        the Changer,

we have come here
to be changed, to be fucked over & fuck
not out of desire but to reform
the dreaded papacy of interstellar spaces
those stellar yokels, these Idis who yoke us down

sub jugum, to come onto earth was to
hunker down under the limbo, to pass
bent before conquistador the latest
with tailfeathers of pure malice
grunting as we bend, he
sweats as we

labor,
        Eros is all about labor
dont you understand,
to love is to be around

love is to be here

this prong to plug us in be plugged
into the colossal keystone cosmos

this house of grass.
This is what you do:
you see her coming & want to climb on
but instead you stand up in front of a crowd of workers
& you say Love it's wonderful but
first we've got to organize

& *then* when you sweat over her in bed
you're breaking those
big sky bosses.

She's made him a steed o' the clear water,
A saddle & bridle o' sand made she;
She's shap'd him into a knight sae fair,
Syne into Mary's kirk-yard rade he.

He's tied his steed to the kirk-stile
Syne wrang-gaites round the kirk gaed he;
And when the Mer-man entered the kirk-door
Awa the sma' images turned their e'e.

—Robert Jamieson, 1806

Wrang-Gaites

Wrong-gaits, wrong-gaits
go back or sun's own
backside
way around the
church to get in,
                then all
the images fall
when this conscious sprite, this
elver-clever lover
lopes
        sideways or rideways
back over the low hedge,
sidles through yew-ways,
hops in,
            is here.

How the devil
half-man-half-
something from the northern sea got
into the schoolyard.
How he prinked

105

the solemn faces of children always
ready to bawl or bleat

how he taught them to laugh
with the terrible
shallow humorless laughter of children.

At the Nottingham Assizes

Is he there?
Can he hear us
when we're hauled before the judge?

Ludd sent us, sir,
we say, Ludd, he said
break these machines
our hands are prisoned in

& get good wages, sir,
for what we make,
& make the baker
sell us penny bread
since all we have's
one penny.

       He said
but we never saw him.
He tells us
in our hearts
how to talk to you now, sir,

though this is a hanging moon
& sixteen men, we knew them,
are bound for Botany Bay, sir,
because of what Ned Ludd
whispered to them in the wood.

The Blue

the cycle
that means around,
means something

around us
we go,
      like the Tuscarora
      who will never,

or the Beothuk,
forever.

I think of John Spicer
alone among the crazies
out at the borderland of conscious life
along the dim summerlands,
that weird bar with blue neon lights where the dead carouse
with whatever he wants, with women for me,
women & blue lights.

Dr Mishra told us round our heads also loins
on contemplating, or set to glow
on our honest northern bourgeois maple
a blue glow
of the "soul-light shrine"
             (Joe Kling was making fun of it,
          Musée Clivette,
      who remembers,
               blue lights for screwing in the
         plush parlor where the
         down there to the shrine,

& Mishra, talking of
love in blue-light,
                    contemplans,
                              who remembers Joe
Kling nailing the Soul
Light Shrine to the
line-up wall of his hard sense,
                    does Burt Britton remember,
surely Ron Kitaj
remembers, we both did
over bagels in Westwood
mourning that good man's suicide)

blue glow of the lamp
he used to seduce
the girl I used
his blue lamp to seduce

until all light was terrible
& stank of will.

*

But I want to redirect
the tide of connection

into *contradiction*
it manages to say,
hey, like apples or pear trees
or men
          quiet in cafes, reading magazines

strictly for the girls of it,
the soul
       vanishes

the soul.   vanishes .   into the shape of things

"All she does is lie around all day
complaining of the light
how little it is, the wind how weak

I would give her our number she would never call."

Sunday Morning

But sitting here
with the individual words
in strong sunlight
waiting for ocean

Sitting here with the individual words
in sunlight waiting for ocean

with the words waiting for ocean

with the ocean

Andre Malraux Dying in a Paris Hospital

Let him pass, let him
into the light that looks at him

then look at the light, let him
say as much to himself
as he has said to me,

let him believe his book.

*

That is the terror of dying
I suppose, that a person forgets
all his works, all his
moonlight conversations   ·

all the clarities
his life work made

all the words
that shadowed the way

now there is no way but away,
this death, this little change.

≡

for Mary

To contend with
that which lies before me. Presents
itself, "self-giving evidence" to
an energy of inquiry
I suppose is myself.

Contend? Not. Not battle,
not handle if to dispose.
Not deal with, as one
solving a problem.
Face. Face & touch

as it seems to go. As it
appears to lie before me
or so moves as to touch
the sources of my supposing
it to be or do so.

This humane problem is to see.
To be submissive
to whole hierarchies of perception
& still face
that which, by being available

to such inspection, is
not for the likes of us.
The likes of me is to see.
To face the forehanded
& see nothing

except what offers itself there.
And then not that.

And then to see.
That is the contention,
ceallach, or strife

from which I am spun out
('named') polarized into
this curious (after all) battle.
Of a *be* & a *see*
such that there must exist

an *A* previous to their order.
And call that *me* (wrong-right)
or some hypostatic enterprise
called He or She (rightwrong)
who gives the evidence

into the tribunal where
it can present itself?
The old story.
It is for example Monday morning.
The oak is asleep.

≡

A wedge in the nature of the world
or clock whose numbers change
frequenter than hands. It may be milk.
What I remembered of you was cloth
I think, my blurred sight
helping itself out by hands. I feel
you coming across countryside. Be.
Be and make me glad.
The old words come again
sure as the fountains of
remorse that is the core of poetry—
that no one has ever loved enough
or left enough, and here we go
singing of it, that sacred absence
which is what I mostly know of God.
To love and to be sure, in that hollow
place inside the solid world
just one word down. Whose tears
are prime salt, our looks our mercury.
Sulfur dreams. We are apart by alchemy,
clock milk, terrible peace.
I wake to you again
and it is always your birthday.

Marian Hymns

I.

Sequences of woods also
coming from Babylon
after this our Exile
Lady bend us home

also with the flex
of your delighted music
we know as muscle
your body moving

open to receive
then closing to ponder
this small utter
gift of our praise

our selves & all our difference.

II.

Some know you as Mary
now & some have spoken
a kind of myth about
how your body in 1950 was it
was taken up to heaven,
the first time those men
ever spoke well of
a woman's body, that
not just your 'grace'
that mystery but your un-
defiled undefiling Body
goes all the way up
& it is heaven where it is.

III.

And great Lucius your votary
said your true name was Isis,
what did he know
except to praise you?

Or Hainuwele lady of Cargo,
Freya of Dawn, white
thighs Morungen saw at morning,
chapel of your presence

& Graves on his knees
before you saw you three times
not each of them accurate
but all of them so

to a nature, Yours,
beyond imagination
but wielding it in us.
Your mouth.

IV.

O you most intricate
lately revealed
as if of cells or that locked
castle called 'genetics'

as if of cells
your grown grace,

bluemantle,
                    our breath,
our blue words
secretly spoken
in your honor
to come close,

                    hard touch,
                    a man to probe your
lucid flesh
o you desire?

V.

To the new-born of it
(to be new born of you
excellent light
sung
through all the maculate phrases
that dim our mind

Sunlight through plastic, shadow is
crystalline.
Diamond dissolved in he-goat's blood,
leper-itch, the horn
lifted against clarity
                    she broke
with her productive
chastity)

        she
out of the strength of her desire
alone
conceived
this fatherless Who
had to have, had
Reality for father

no realler really than She,
spoken
in the arrovo
the vast liɡ   .

VI.

Our blue words mantle you in a fur
of obscene airs, these songs of ours, our 'graces'
by which when we hail you comes light of the mother
kind as girl, cream skin, unimpeachable
dignity: a clean smell. From the arroyo
up before breakfast, when the air is
what we call 'deep inside you,'
'grammar of all living,' 'your mouth,' 'taste
of your tongue' in our stammering mouths,
our tendernesses, our deft deliveries forgive.
Who want you so much. Who man you.
Who in our simplest of all meanings
would nail you to the sky with the cock of our praise.

To Aphrodite

Not the easiest things
but the easiest
things
    the rolling off this morning
not knowing

not knowing.
I am & then again
girled with apprehension of

the simplest things.
Where are you
Lydian
    when I need you now?

Come as once before
from the darkest gold-entablatured
house of my head
to stand
    before me in the public air

sturdy wings of your
whirring around you

unsettling the dust/

the ground I stand on.

Studies from the Mishnah.

I.

Can the shadow of a menstruating woman defile?
can the shadow of a woman defile?
can the shadow defile?
                  Can the shadow of a woman
bring blessings? Can the shadow of a tree
drop fruit on my plate? *Responsa:*
            It has.
          It was in a city far to the west.
They were figs.   She still is.

What is it the shadow could bless or defile?
Is it a thing? Is it a wall
shaped like a word, a field all stretched out
easy in front of your house?
Does the water boil?
If the shadow falls in boiling water
will the coffee taste of a woman?
Is there anything anybody can do
that does not taste of her or him?
If he paints a wall is her shadow in it?
Answer: If he speaks a word she's in it.
If she speaks a word it is single,
it means he should tell her the whole story.
Eat most of the fig.
Sleep with her even then
while the blood of imagination reddens her thighs &
defiles them both into a blessing.
How can that be? Is a field
the same as a house? They live there. Can a wall
have a memory, can a cup of coffee

say the morning prayer?
Can anything at all
pray for us in the silence of hearing?
Talk to her. Tell her the whole field
across which you have come
remembering her some of the time.
Does the memory of a woman defile the day?
Does a shadow of a word defile a field
when people speak there in the thin shade of a fig tree?
When he is telling her the whole story?
Does only a piece of a fruit defile?
Whereas the whole fig? The whole body?
If the shadow falls on a mind will it be a woman?

Studies from the Mishnah

III.

[*Note:* the Mishnah is the first writing-down of the Oral Law of
the Jews. It is a sudden text, then, where speech had been. This
third study is motivated by the triliteral root D-B-R, which has
(at least according to the old lexicographers) the 'root-meaning'
of *behind*, then of setting one thing after another, thus arrang-
ing, thus speaking coherent words, thus words so arranged, or
any words, or any thing at all. As 'speak' or 'word' or 'thing' the
root most frequently incarnates.]

(DBR)

Behind
this book
I want to get behind
this book this thick
thing this afterlude
this thick belated thing this thick
this book
   I want
to get behind this book this thick
thing spoken,
    back
to the Oral Law
they say came before
& talks behind this book.
But *they say* it only in a book, this thick
replacement for a savage breath
or lover's idle soft breathing left
a minute later still ringing in the ear
how soft she said
     whatever it was she said—

& in this Spoken
Law thank God
the message can get lost.
Back behind the book is a beforeness.
Before the thing written thickly in the book
is a breath breathing. Before the breath
is a breather. That means a pause
or silence or a rest. Or one who pauses
her mouth half-open at my ear
about to speak. Or not. Or let
the message loose into its breath.

The law
breathed its last
into a book.
Now it lasts
instead of breathing.

I want to get behind this book I find her breathing.

If the blood falls on his left hand it is invalid,
but R. Simeon says it is valid.

If any thing,
then this thing.

If what I mean
falls on the left
I leave it
or am left there

:with no strength.
It means: it doesnt count.

I count
the blood falling through my arteries
seeking the borders of my ancient kingdom

finding the limit
& past that the
place is You.

Or it is no place. The blood falls
I lift my left hand
& let it fall on the small of your back.
My hand calls you soft there, calls the skin meek.
My hand falls.
What it feels
I understand as brightness. It counts
(says Simeon bar Yochai, the master of lights,)
every touch counts when you do it.

*

But a blood is of a slaughtered thing
a sacrifice, a use-it-up
poured
     from a thing to a thing. The hand
interrupts the fall.
         To hold the blood & aim it,
sprinkle the altar
with this rain
     had been inside
a living thing now just a thing.
          The thing burns.
The blood
     falls through my hands.

Meditation on a Well-Known Phrase of St Augustine

After intercourse every living thing is sad
he said,
        knowing more about *tristis* than *coitus*,

remembering, remembering.
O my Christ how did they blur you so
into an enemy of ecstasy when
all Your life You stood outside
every possible self, any
consensus they gave you,
                & every day
You were rising up to heaven from them, from Yourself
ascending into a precise exaltation,

that is to the real. Then came Christians
to redistribute the real over the sad consensus,
where ecstasy is the enemy of economy &

Augustine stood by the last silken (real silk,
remember, warm from her) bedside
of his last, his very last lover &

that was the end of it. The sadness of leaving her
he redistributed over the act of being inside her.
He built the Church of St Sorrow, the grief
was the last thing he remembered of the silk.

"And though you go (she said) to China or the Antipodes
or to the Castle behind the Northern Lights
you will find bed there, Bed, & it will be
a fine place, & the same place, ever, your only

dignity this joy you'd lose in leaving."

In Florence, in Piero's Time

after Vasari

There came one day a heavy fall of snow.
They brought Michelangelo to the courtyard
where the servants with fresh straw brooms
had swept the rarity into one great heap,
lifting & packing with slim summer shovels.
A waist-high heap of snow then, clean,
stood like an altar to be dressed for Mass.
Dry crystals sparkled in the sun.

Because snow is such a fleeting thing
he chose to make a fugitive, a Gaulish nude
fleeing from Romans after a small unannaled
catastrophe in the wintery Ardennes.
(Gauls always came into battle naked
save for the twist of pure gold round the neck.)
The weary boy has been running since dawn
& stands now panting for breath, sweat
actually icing on his sides as they heave.
He looks up to his old midmorning sun,
same one that blazes down now on the snow.
Am I cruel to make him naked in the cold?
What grace this fugitive medium!
How short a time he is a graceful child—
grows hard, grows stiff—then Death takes him.

The sculptor's eyes ache from brightness,
no stone was ever fierce like this;
he mixes ashes in olive oil, smears some
on cheekbones & round his eyes to dull the glare.
Then he must wash his hands to keep his matter clean.
They bring him gloves he won't put on:

130

his hands prefer the pain of intimate touch.
Till the boy is all there, this thrown-back forearm
shielding his eyes. Then for a long time the sculptor's
shadow shields the boy's perfected face.

Surgical Piano

Surgical piano the tune
neatly lifted away from the music till
penetrating furthest abscesses of thought
the surgeon abolishes the complexity he thinks

he is left
with something bare somehow impressive
young women swoon when they look at it
but turn away for example to Chopin
leaving their cut-off locks & lunar blood
at the shrine of rubato which
brings all formal things to life they think

I have not been clear
it is not about women & men not about pianos
it is not about music it is something
happens inside the head when
at morning I think

but music is
& this is not about anything I think
not about anything
but it gets there
the way baserunners or pianists do up & down the
scales: ladders
going somewhere & coming back
angels in moonlight
the girl next door
eloping in a cartoon.

Of Poetics

And it would be that way with the two of them
the whole winter
sometimes talking sometimes
he thought it was poems they were writing or she
was writing in him
from all that distance

spoken
out of the common snow that this year
had its way with the whole seaboard
there was no hope
after all
of being different
they loved each other & were far

she was writing in him
& sometimes they came onto the paper
like snowmobile tracks found at morning
up their hill theirs no
longer & not even a memory
of some hard noises in the night
to show what but they knew full well what
had gone that way

that poetry
is as brutal as such machines
& leaves tracks on a less perishable surface
from which the person or personality of whoever was driving
has long ago been able to disappear
back in his private ranch-house.

Canto CXXX

Find the city
locked
in the design:
        a cloverleaf
    held aloft
        by some Patrick
   Here
is the Trinity.
        Non est non est non est
                she
is a tissue of Negation,
        Lady, tell me
who is God? Abscondite.
        Where is she?
—Why are you so quiet?
—I am not much today. It goes
through me. I have
nothing to say.
—These are the silences.

    From them
    the only
    is made music

    belongs to us.
I mean the only proper music
is that cast around our own silences.
In this sand. Process
of the lost word.

Our breath
          how long & how pretermitted,
given
     whole or broken into
song silence. The way.
And I have tried, Jesu, Jesu the
ways
     I have tried.
The rumors the rumors
          the stammers the stammers—
rode
into the little town just at dark
the one restaurant
found . . .
          has there ever been a lover?

First Jewish Sonnet

Who is it who comes to me from the Sabbath
dry-eyed covered with care? Who wakes for me?
To be born is to be Jewish. My Lord & My Lady were so,
I chose their clarity in all this general forest.
The woods of Are. I am grateful. Dark linen
of the bed, shadows of earlier passion, you smell me
of us both. Sound of far trickling woke me,
as if a pipe were freezing or thawing. Or water spoke
its own name & woke me. My eyes are dry. Was I trying
to see in the dark as I slept? Read, & there was no text?
Who is the text speaks out of the Sabbath
& reads me awake, dry-eyed till the morning star,
like King David above whose bed a lute was hung
that woke him with its music when the north wind blew?

Second Jewish Sonnet

I still hear the water, old house in wind.
She speaks in me still, from when she tongued me
to attention & spoke all his lessons, held me
till my male spirit flew into her & left
a shuddery irritable midnight male,
satisfied, sleepy, wanting to read, too tired to.
How ungracious to my perfect lover
who forgives me into the privacy of her sleep.
And I sleep, as if a love had ended by being so full.
See, it is as they say: if the Sabbath came every day
men would keep no Sabbath. To get what I want
& to go sleep from it, terror of the empty night
that I could mean so little & be so normal
& fall convenient among the satisfied.

Third Jewish Sonnet

"How fine is this tree!" he said, "this field"
he said—& it was as if a sin
against his own life, to interrupt his study
of the book of praises
                                    to prize that tree.
Melons grow in the field, & deep long beets.
Each leaf of the tree has words on it,
he dozes in wonder—did he write them,
just read them? Do his hands still work?
The tree's name is lost, for all the words
he can make out of the leaves. It is late.
The road he walked on meant to be a book.
"The law!" he said, "this blossom up out of all of us
when we were ready. I dont understand.
I read my way into its hands."

There Is a Room Where It Is Rare

There is a room where it is rare.
It is a window or a door
or a story coming across the water
of when he was coming or he came.
There is no harm in it
except what you find there, I hid it
between the fine strands of her hair
teased almost silver. It was raining
& she carried unopened an umbrella.
He was one of the just ones
whose hopes had nothing to do with the night.
Their worth works. Hard to say,
but even when they sleep.
She didnt see them, found
herself under awning or marquee
with a closed red umbrella wet in her hand.
I have dreaded beauty all my days
its power on me.
How when her lover
knocked plangent at her door
she went on staring out the window,
down of her cheek nibbled by the rough silk curtain
beige or yellow. Then the banging stopped.
There was no sound on the staircase
so she wasnt sure he had actually gone
till she saw him, in the usual Estonian scarf,
turning out of the courtyard onto the street.
There are always fewer subways where the rich live.
Went later to the zoo where she watched seals.
Their relationship to dogs. A photograph
I certainly never saw. Sweet popcorn in boxes,
smell of weasels. "It is or isnt, I did

let him go. There is no chance of his return."
She lets it bring her home to the fireplace.
The broad piano or the gull on the windowsill.
Pigeon, of course. Anyone can sometimes forget.
The fire was set for the rest of the night
the way the damper was fixed. Her guess
didnt really count. Even the phone ring
she not to answer. Some verb
she couldnt remember & didnt do.

Turangalila Meditation

Luxury of metal quality, I want a gong
to beat inside you—making love
is also getting ready,
stripping away all cleverness.
All things are clear in her hand, she is more
than her hands, her parts
are quick births & we come to speak.

There is not much to remember.
Glory is always part of the
weather we're part of,
roaring in the zoo,
holy animals who lead us into trouble,
'get us in dutch,' that is Touch
& all it leads to
a woman gives it to a man by taking.

Credo in unam deam, Matrem
omnipotentem, creatricem
of all things sensible & unconscious,
maker of heaven & heaven in earth.

The fat space of the cathedral chants her dark
litanies, the cool grey stone light of the Lady Chapel
lets me sit down. There is rest here. The traffic
is not far. I hear it
through the ideal blue of the ogival windows,
glass stained color of consciousness, love her,
everywhere I have gone was for her sake.

Or the truth of it, the only thing I ever sought
was women, the woman,
                         everything else was at hand
useless until I found her she found me.

I dont want to write love songs, dont want
to write "I" any more, write "want" any more.
It is here. It makes noise. It is touch
& bent over your head on the pillow as the light itself
bent over the earth & slipped down into evening.

The Archive

Hair in old photograph

Young Bolshevik
caught
by Denikin's army,
                    his fine hairs, fuzz,

dead sixty years

the hair
in focus.

The Runaway Slave

Open this window.
Tell the captain
I have departed his crummy hacienda
for a lengthy sojourn in Aphrica
where he cant tell his
mumps from my mambas.
Leave him my contract
scribbled in the breezy jive of old reporters.
I know there will be midnights when
I miss the captain & lick my scars
reflective as December.
Tell him I'm moving quick & sure,
there are rivers around the piranhas,
dare him to follow me in socks.

*

I really want to be so obvious
& leave a dump of shit
thirty feet from the campfire
in the direction I wasnt heading.
He'll figure it out.
He knows how to speak palmtree,
sapodilla, mangrove.
To me those are just words
in books I am too ignorant to read.
I hear the dogs mumbling at night
dreaming their masters' education
close to the dying driftwood fire.
My masters! Tell him to run
as if my feet were sweet napoleons
flaking to meet him.

*

This raft is made of shoes.
The boat that leaves for Aphrica
takes much persuasion.
I have to tell lies to the sails
& suck the oarlocks clean.
I have to trust—
& that is hardest, to float
through the oilspill & coconuts & junk
of all the islands
spent into this trivial current
that carries me home.

*

I am a part of this ever-returning economic mess,
a unit of labor lost, a scum of profit
thick on my heels. I am a part
of money! Tell him he can see me
only as a hump or a hope
on his metaphysical horizon.
I will be safe in jungle & he will find me
when he finds his Grail.
I am his last myth, and I am gone.

Texts: 32   [Hymn to Phrygian Aphrodite]

Who would speak well of the gods,
who by the red silk of the martyrology
nibbled with gold thread should
prick out narratives of the gods' great servants
dangled the structure
                    in worm-web,
build the book, & bind it,
in textile text, true to the deep suppose.

Where was the story coming from
when that shapely or formal wave
lifted randomly against the beach
bringing Her with it, breath of a once-before,
she whose Descent
                    is only from the Father
motherless then, mild, open-fisted as daylight
stood out of the foam
                    to make me perfect,
She said, heal, she said.

I was in terror of her wetness, her water
would dye my life, my whole manhood
was a dread of what she was coming.
But she calmed me into my future:
Stay, I will not go,
I will be with you
longer than children.
Spin the red text.
You will not wake from me
nor the world from you, knot over knot
tightened, hyparxis, the node of Now.
I need you
for some reason.

She said & was silent
who came to me. I had been
She said on her mind,
thus a place
to which she came
by thinking.
Something of me was obstinate to sea, a solid,
obedient to her mind.
So I was land, book. So open
or closed the text reads on. Land
calmed into her arrival, the birds
hung motionless in the air, her doves my
humdrum sparrows. Hung in the weaving,
filigree, what's it called,
the tissue of our consciousness
shared or not parted, imparted.

*

Later putting her clothes back on she
looked further inland: Time
was what they forced there from the ground,
then seasons spill
thick in the gunny-sacks
of seed. Sow in February, reap in moonlight.
Who would serve her better
would be, as I am, bitter,
of thought & to the taste,
what we had done each other with this lingering.
The birds on the binding,
metal-plumage, tender,

                    lost overhead.

My Correspondence with Hemingway

Dear friend, he began

Poetry is no proof against suicide
but I thought fiction was

Poetry was too beautiful & I—

"little green flies
up
out of the future

I breathe an ocean
wider than ours is"

or then again I wrote

"the weft of things"

*

I woke early to this conceit
the snow was,
                        after a springlike week
after such a winter.
Maybe Rick's ice-boats at Barrytown
will act out a scared opera for me,

up early, before the sun.
Later in the week,
                        the ice-boats at Bellport
on my first shore.

Landing from the midwest
the small jet came in over Staten Island.
I could see all over Brooklyn,
Marine Park, Sheepshead Bay,
Gerritsen Beach, dark arrow
of Flatbush Avenue headed north
—Nativity

"I could see" means "I saw"

You could see means
You have to listen to me

A minute later I saw the Colosseum
& the little woods south of it where we
first came ashore. First shore.
Exules filii Hevae I explained,
or why the Grail, this
stone of exile.

Stone
(rock)
to which
we're exiled.

This earth our Alcatraz

—means Albatross
a seabird's laughter
over our aching rock.

This earth
is exile.
This planet
is the Grail.

Drink up & go.

*

And what of those letters from Hemingway, how he tells me how hard it
was, not to write, but to be content with prose. "Prose invents, and what it
leaves behind is all I really wanted. The look of a place after the place has
been described. The feel of a woman after there is no problem with her.
After description every animal is sad."

That's where that letter ended, one he wrote from Montreal one weekend
late in life. In my infrequent responses I tried to be clear with him that the
life a person lives also inscribes itself in the written text—by a "somehow"
not yet deciphered. (That was my young man's pompous way of saying it.)
This "somehow" makes the writing of youthful contingency more poig-
nant, however flawed, than the decorous perfections of middle-life. "The
only chance is chance? Is that what you're saying?" he wrote. But no, I
answered, it is as your own fables seem to portend, the only chance is *risk*.
The only book worth writing is one you dont know how to write.

The War Criminal

I did not disbelieve
strongly enough in coercion.
The sun kept coming up,
I kept feeling forgiven.

Even the soft rain
was meant for me.
I had signs.
My world had meanings,
not morality.
Maybe that is why
some Jews felt
sorry for me at my trial:

I knew
how to take everything
personally.
They had their Law
but I had only signs,

signs & cruel superiors
insisting what I do.
I suppose I was guilty—
& that's the puzzle,
that it is even now
just a supposition,

an inference
from the rope they looped
around my neck,
from the swarm of terror
up my chest as my
body rushes down.

                    Now

what is the Earth
trying to tell me?

The Missionary

It is about
Time,
that Object
of all Subjects

I smell her
even from here

my sermon tells.

What is it called
on this side
of transcendence?
The river
has many names,
flows down the Dead Mountains
its gorge cut through
one single emerald;
debouches onto the Elephant Plains
ripe with mandolins,
oil of garter.
Plough-snouted stern-wheelers
bong upriver from Lake Whisky.
It is agreeable.
It is a country
suitable for your money
give it to me.

By its solid pragmatism
rescue me
from the embraces
of the tempestuous Warner Bros jungle queen
I dream of every night
whose jewish buttocks
gleam with irresistible radiance through
the vascular over-runs of our lowlands—
she pees in reeds.
The sight of her
becomes my Qabbalah—
save me
from her clarity.
The outer world
is grim there too:
the border of the Soviet Congo
runs not far from our German
Settlements (Reformed)—
I have been shot at
from their sniping towers,
ladies, I, the humblest
whose whole life has been
to translate the gospels
into the dialects of Thigh,
Cushion, Soft-back,
Clitorix & Hip,
that form the great phylum of Lap,
language of the Grail.
(Of the Gods themselves
who come to see Her
in my mind!

I abase myself
before Her wilful estrangement
from any political
reality!) O ladies
give me money!
Unglue my passion!

I am the unforgiven,
the priest in paradise,
a voice beneath an orchid leaf,
python in my pocket,
a feast of whys.
O ladies listen,
I fear to lose your attitudes,
your audient collar-bones, ladies,
bones of your faces, cheeks,
necklaces, soft way you sit
on slatted folding chairs
or sumptuous in bentwood pews
o it has been so long,

I bring them all home
into the endless jungle
listen to me,
I need your hearts
for mine is failing
at the incessant news,
every bird brings it,
all my life I never knew it,
Earth's just a colony of the moon.

I mean this momentary warmth
of fleshy sense
is trapped in an abstract everywhere
of cold philosophy
means nothing but Meaning
everywhere & no caresses
Give me money for the sake
of the original Subject
of all transcending
that brought us here
to make my broken lecture
while the jungle grows
& no man knows it better than I
who am all growth & no constraint.
Listen, loins! The awful lions
conjugate the only verb I know,
their teeth in flashing conversation,
their hearts asleep.

*The Table Drank the Milk

[The sentence is offered to us by a linguist as "ungrammatical," or not normal.]

What would Simon Magus say
or Helena that girl of his, that
Tyrian exile her skirt
always falling round her feet
deep shadow in her bellybutton,
earth's gnomon, earth's center?
Would she know the norm of normal,
would she be the lithe
twist of sense
                gives light
in the heart of any grammary?

She said: *I am me.*
I drink the milk.
I am the table
you want me to be.

I sit in myself.
I last & all the others fade,
even my name
becomes a trade:
all the lovely slutty lonely
girls are Helenas
who mean so much & no man listens.

The milk
is my mister's, this milk
I drink with my mother's mouth.
I hold it in.

157

I last with a kind of endurance
called Dancing.

She is naked now
except for what her hair hides
if that's hiding
that is so bright & various falling
down around her like dark milk.
How did she get to be a table?
She rested & was relevant.
Men counted on her,
write on her, eat from her lap.
I can be anything you choose.
I am who lets you choose
me or any other, forever.
I drink what you call milk
I let it slip
down in me & around me
till it reaches what you call earth.

Then she tells me everything but I dont listen.

tell me love how bodies pray
is it with architectures or languages learned
is it not rather with their soft bodies
pressed against seats in the dark pews
or hardening slowly under the drone
of the endless ritual of your beauty?

Let the Nobody who cares
about all the sad smilies
butt-ended on barstools
mirrored in forty year old mirrors
reflect
that all our loneliness is for Her
the peace of the World.

Gypsies

On our block Gypsies
used to come Saturday,
preferring to bilk the man of the house
on his day off from being anybody.
They were tinkers, ineffective,
unreliable, clever with some language
not even they could actually speak.
I still see his stubbled chin, skin of his face
color of bread.

≡

Not I think what I
find through the window
when the rain sky cracks
in high wind to the
beloved sun

         come again
I said there is a cut
inside the piece called
'day' such that
the inside is bigger
than the outside,
like a metaphor in Dante

to choose an example
from the litter left
around the room
topology of chance
(maybe) but surely
topography of what there
simply is

        you delude yourself.
Red sky at morning
sailors take
exactly that the storm
of rain is over
the wind begins now

If the ship is a tree
it will shed its leaves.

Texts: 25   [The Philosopher's Stone]

"the original self-giving evidence"   (Derrida on
the stone   Husserl)
          Deucalion
cast over his shoulder in a sack
a sack
          but lost it, going,
going
          where Deucalions go
when they lose it,
                    the just man?
                              query, the stone?
It comes back to me
from my childhood
how one day I heard or read more likely read
of The Philosopher's Stone
& was filled with subtle excitement
that did not die, that quivers inside me
like Sappho's to this day fire
& I knew that this
this stone whatever it was
was the business of my life
so quietly that day, in sunlight, afternoon,
no weirder time than that, out of
a comic book, contracted.
A contract
          signed,
Mitra or Miθra abogado of that promise, guard
(guide) of that oath—
an oath
the breath
of my excitement
swore for me
ever after.

163

So lightly taken are they,
these steps which are defining gestures,
measures,
the Feel that is a road
ever after to have walked on
scrupling even for one week to leave—
I did not, for whatever virtue
hidden in the idleness of time,
I did not leave.
There is also a stone-like inertia
which is the stone
& a way to the stone
to be carried.
But it is hard to be carried, hard to go
& the going is, & the go.
Lord of the Contract.
The stone
marker at the edge of the field, I had found
a way at the stone.
The stone
was immediate.
Gives light & makes change
obedient to will,
makes change & the coins
hit the floor like the subway rolling
& the stone gets into the crannies of things with its powder
& the powder clones fox-face in heather.
It is smart. It persuades
all things to be of its intention, be of like mind
& it is the field where all things happen.
It is moral by persuasive power, it coaxes
the facts of such matter it finds into thinking as it does,

stone-wise, suddenly a good deal brighter, an amazement

& not gold. I did not care that the dictionary
if ever I got around to looking it up
would tell me the Stone turned,
turned base metals to gold, it was the first
I heard a metal could be base
when my Uncle Joe with such skill had made
a stainless steel coin bank riveted shut
ground down smooth & very bright, impregnable,
what was this gold? I did not care for this gold.
Gold was a field for mercury to run on
& turn the air black
so that the light of flesh, of women on my mind
all round me in the immense then the greatest
city, flesh-light would focus & be the whole
light of existence, that sex would be the absolute

since my heart & my body craved that singularity.
It blazes at midnight
(do I mean the sex, the stone, the sun its congener?)
seen through the exploded lexicon of the consensus,
fading renaissance of our perspectives, tattered
geometries of how things are supposed to work
but none of it works
except the stone,
marker at the edge of the field,
edge
        of that experience:
                            the world as sign, then.
And I am suddenly religious as any, to find
the proper glue for this population I am,

                              religion
the binding together again
          by the power of this stone
that shattered person myself,
                       bind
bone into blood-sea, brain over arquebus on these shoulders
holy,
        this weaponer, this Man
I persist to want to call me
from the bottom of my call,
                         Lord of the Stone.
And how could there ever not be a way there,
when the stone is self-disclosing
& opens on a self
waiting
          to be empurpled with the late flowers of time,
item,
        to grow among men & be god.

Or what he did was throw it away
bone of his bones
his own
          & his right to cast,

so that all generations come from
that lucky toss
grew from his bones,
plucked from his backbone
miscast in the story's image as
a wallet slung round his neck.
And when you find a stone throw it behind you throw it behind
you: it may have been the wind hissing past his

ears must have been good in its own way,
stone of the bright brow
that lit the path
through the dark of an imageless
condition,

        after the deluge, light of his head.
The gods
      broken into the pieces that are us.

Arctic Embryo

found beneath a lamen of three-year ice
salt almost squeezed out, the juice
when melted down was fresh. The little glob
had sort of life. We warmed it
by sewing it into the thigh of a cat, later
when it grew into the arm of a man.
It thought its way down the vein,
it was translucent as rabbit ears,
it talked & it wanted & would kill to get it
but even after birth refused to say its name.

Easter

Come back from wherever it has been
it is the name of it
frost on Easter morning
the slow light.
I wanted to say everything,
be back from the tomb in time—
wanted, & was so slowly unafraid
that all these years can pass
on my way to being
clear about where it has been.
Clear
       about anything

            □

How much to care
about how she sits on a chair.
About the silences,
barriers I have allowed
into existence. Built them
by inattention.
The being-passive does all the work,
imbecile giants.
Unanalyzable wound!
               To wake again
               no wiser.
I moan at the gates of my lost life,
come out Lord
but I cannot touch him
ler her touch me.

□

What is the tomb & what
was the Crucifix?

The sad permissions of everyday,
answered the bird from the ground.

□

To stand outside while it's still 29°
sun not yet touching the thermometer but close,
the air spacious, relieved
after its confinement,
having given birth to the Awful day.
And what if 'to focus' means
'to be trapped,' or 'be specific'
'be locked in?'
            I am of that company
of travellers who mostly linger,
amateurs of windows, who can still conceive
no torture worse than a prison.

□

Prisoners not of fact but of opinion.
We are locked
in description.

Harrowing of Hell:
when he took the description away.

170

□

I grew up learning & almost experiencing
that he woke up into bread.
This bread could be eaten & I ate.
To my surprise, it didnt stave off appetite;
I was always hungry. I knew later
from the Discourse with the Woman at the Well
that I had missed the point. I am not sure
what the point is, but nothing I have ever experienced
made me want to stop experiencing.
I have not yet learned humility
in the face of my inadvertence.
It is still a shock that I can't have everything.
I can have everything.
Here I say it, round with proof,

& Faust drops the poison bottle
having tricked the poor Devil
into once more taking an interest
in the predictable enterprises of men,
we cheap desirers. Sometimes I feel
the sun itself is tricked to rise.
And those birds that woke me
at the first full light
are suborned witnesses of a resurrection
about which they no longer remember
exactly what they saw or sang.
As if that would be the true story.
Memory is never right.

□

Forget it, by definition.
O world my binary!
Christos anesti!—That much at least
we are given, we Jews for Jesus,
he's up! he's up again
like Finnegan, yellow-head
turfed out of the
bog at the back of the Pole.
How little it was
to rise again,
how little it was to die
compared to the terror of
living a lifetime here with us,
locked in this planet.
We live here but he knew better.
We all know better,
says the shadow on the scratchy lawn.

□

How little it is to live or die
compared to knowing something, knowing,
that money of easy eternity—
& I have no knowledge
except what I make up,
poor Easter-robert, poor white flabby Ram.

□

By now the sun has taken it off,
poverella rugiada!
I mourn the frosts of the world,
the hard the bright, crystal,
to which only the softness of flesh bears
the cross of meaningful comparison.

□

Now the season of between begins
that feeds us amply
& all those are harvested
that we call bread.

□

Why should I wake on Easter with that soft
doughy memory, a girl's body in a hard place?
The breathless comparisons!
that the world as we construct it
is hard, unforgiving, as if a sullen wife it were,
fierce at some plausible adultery.

□

What did we do to the world
Parmenides did not do first,
or salient Buddha knowing it to bits?
I chopped down this tree
ten thousand times before

173

& always it comes back,
madera we seek, y pintura, y cristales,
lumber yard & all those bright
betrayals prettify our house—
crystal, I mean window,
let light in!
          Let our darkness out
to roll with the rabbits in their forms,
soft fur, tiny bones, heart full of terror.

□

I didn't see the woodchucks by the road,
those risers, looking up with their goofy
old-gentleman look, stupefied
by the crazy cars that kill them.
By now they should be out & various
along the Taconic. Is it the weather?
Or has the government abolished them,
signing a Decree against the Unprotected?

□

It is always the name of it.
It has no windows
& dust is eaten there.
I want to be so good to my friends
but my dreams tell me
she is like a typewriter, dirty,
international, on sale.
I can have her. Olympia,

taupe & tan, my dancing girl, d'Hoffman,
glittering rubati of her frail clockwork:
this girl pretends to be mechanical,
runs down, flops forward stiff from the waist.
Is it her machine or her pretense
that horrifies her lover so?
It is hell. I died
into this place where her dance runs down.
I opened my Missal to find
the texts of resurrection, found
the lamentable mystery of her wheels & gears.

□

Dust our food, a catalogue of lusts
set beside our places: Read to eat.
And as we read at our separate tables,
trying to prop the nurseryman's ads
& the bookseller's lists & the *Times*
against the cold toaster
without knocking over
the wilting daffodils she'd forgotten to discard,
there came a sound of beating on the door,
far away, & then the crash of wood & bronze,
walls falling in. Brick dust & mortar
settled on our food. We heard
a trumpet braying on short-wave
& then the house was full of businessmen
unpacking samples, exchanging overcoats,
signing documents with ballpoint pens.
Then a rush of big men in bright uniforms,
sunglasses winking at us with perhaps

175

unintentional bonhommie. Then he was there
& the walls fell outward
& the prison we were in became the world.
The world became space & space became
time & the time was right & through
the loving mouth of time we climbed
groaning & exulting out & were free.

□

While Christ was ostensibly dead or sleeping in the tomb
he was in fact busy harrowing hell.
Waking the afterlife to be before. Returning
all those lovers to the light.
                              To the timid
he gave terror, their best weapon.
To the confident he gave women
to search the limits of their certainty.
To the wicked he gave lots of choices.

To the good he gave themselves.

□

I want to tell the truth of my life
to keep them from listening.
I have kept from doing the best things,
busy with the good.
It is inexcusable, since it is verbal
& I should have known, being a book.
I go back to my shelf & lurk,

part of the Dusty Army of the Ages
whose war may never come.

☐

Touch things,
touch them kindly
not gently

touch them
till they're touched
& you can tell.

☐

And to whom
do I presume
to offer
such adolescent wisdom?
To that pre-teen my Heart
huge physically in my chest
yet of questionable moral volume,
a mystery, a hearth of God.

☐

And if the heart
comes out on easter
& cleans the fallen
potato stix from the back
seat of the car

& tries
        to dry
the soaked front floorboards
in cold sunlight
& finds its suspicions confirmed
about the daffodils
& succeeds in adjusting the seatbelt post
& even gets the cotter pin back in place
& dumps the drekh in a coke carton
& lives in America, dreams Egypt,
wakes up typing on her flesh,
if it remembers & remembers to forget,
if it forgets, if it goes
in the Heart Boat to Thebes Up There
& counts all afternoon columns at Karnak,
rosary of emissions, semen in the head,
high heat, palpitate, drum in her honor,
if it leans on the car & looks at the sky
& imagines the princesses of light there
dancing invisible now drenched with daylight,
can it be said to have come forth from the tomb?
Or is the tomb
forever
so much
part of its story
it carries it with it
wherever it goes?

The Agony in the Garden

Know the date by the dirt on it.
Were we ever not too tired to protest
the sad machine we sweat to run?
Were we ever?
There is a football field
on which a better game is played.
The geometers assemble
        with their cones & pies
& sit down with geometresses,
        medrésses, matrices
        for their lunch.
Above them three sparrow hawks
        tow a campaign promise:
They believe in number! it said.
Lions are roaring with finite appetites.
The Kill Quality. It falls
from heaven & is measured.
Their lips (only the humans
have lips in this picture)
are plumb-lines that measure war.
They talk.
            How close they are,
sitting in their forms like rabbits.
They are conscious of little but what goes on
in the associative echo-chambers of their endless thought,
hence conscious of nought.
Steam-powered floats come up the sand
bearing peonies from Alexandria.
The driver is a woman who seems
uncomfortable in daylight—who is she?
The geometers realigned their strings.
It is noon in Thebes, they cry, *great*

Amon falters in the merciless light.
A dog-like thing runs to question them:
Who is she exactly? What is the proportion
of a sphere to the cylinder it's scribbled in?
(The Cynomorph is a classifier. You count in him.)
The people speak. *It is noon now*
in Jerusalem & the seacoast here
convulsed with cloud—does time run back?
There is silence in Gethsemani. *An olive*
bitter red, bitter on my lips.
But only the language has lips.

Blue Nude

Blue nude first thing we saw together
a kind of sensory pool let myself just this once
move through
                        you, in you more than in them
the images.
                    What I wanted was your hips in my hands
guiding you onto me
                            answering scrupulously what I feel
across the room you feeling from me. Cold museum mix
kiss in the corner of your mouth with later my
teeth on your right breast,
                            see how they paint that.
Is there anything you care for except making love?
Learn that language, let the heart be sacred that way,
man in his ordinary clothes his heart flaming through qiana
to you. Take him. Me.
                    The naked. We are the naked
& all the rest is lie.

2.

Most mild sound through the cloud of unseeing
suddenly want. Want you. This
composition folds back into one's hands:
                            To live
with never a sense of loss. That is the way.
To be always driving, savage from this moment, new born, wise.
Outside spring rye hopefullest green. Hope
will not do. It must be red. It must burn the museum instead.

3.

If I could be grateful to the highest star
& share the beliefs gone mute now in the heart,
ashamed in mind but living still, a sort of Lazarus,
my faith would grow again. Why not to touch you?
Are you afraid you'd belong to me? I have no vault,
I am one earth of knowledge & desire & possession
unpossessed. Everything I teach
can be forgotten. It is clean. The blue
nude swims across our common mind. I want you,
all of you, once to have felt me. This hurried art
to say it all.
              The greed of experience is a second star
shines above the manger of our birth, new horoscope
fallen among shepherds who came to praise
the holy animal in us before those kings
stagger in from dying Persia to praise our souls.

4.

Good sullen self-intent hard work that makes us monsters.
Learn so much passion the broad-leaved Matisse
trembles at such intensity—only soft pre-war colors
flaking down from a temporary world. Your eyes
burn at it, mild eyes, sacrifice all the things you see
on some weird altar.
              Like the woman you saw once down below
trapped in a gesture, subway, bending, touching her toes
alternately, eternally.

182

I feel the squeeze
in her loins when she does that,
                              twist of middle, animal
to whom we come.
                    These stupid places where people move
& art is motionless,
                    how can that work ever?
                                        There is a night
to hide us coming now,
                    the star
of everything we ever did
                    burns low in your body now.
Deep inside the image there is time for everything.

The Woman Who Heard Horses Scream at Dusk

for N.N.

Every night. Every.
She heard them first when she was watching
the tops of her white thighs.
Every night they spoke again.
Near her room others hear them too.

Bakers turn away from their cool ovens.
It is dark inside jetplanes
grounded on broken runways.
Nothing goes. All the workers
have gone to their houses
as arranged.

She is alone
except for the neighing horses.
They come from the stable on the cobbled mews
halfway between her street & mine.
They come from the old churchyard where they graze.
They come from the cellars of brick houses
where silent children won't eat their supper.
They come from under the streets
where their hooves clatter on the wet rock of old sewers.

They come from something she holds in her hands.
They come from the sea.

mazy moon
four a.m.

there is nowhere
in the sky

cold twist
of a heartless road

my own, my own
crooked mile.

At the well bent low

a maiden
offering drink

This is not
            she warned
a natural water

& I drank.

Kill what is only
natural in me

I begged of it,

leave only the yeast
by which a better matter
will be lifted.

And what is that
                she said
but the empty cup?

The Talk of Angels

There is a southern village where a girl
sits soft on a stool by the fire.
She turns an old schoolbook, sees
frizzy haired rapists from the Solomons,
cannibals, heathens, somethings
she cant name. Her bottom's a little
broader than the seat; though she is slender
she seems now opulent, master
of many choices, where will she go?
Where the whales spout or the citrons grow,
cypresses' relief at noon, señoritas
paddle in lagoons, men drunk all day
on fruity wines & spit-fermented beer?
The wedge of her opened book
presses in her lap, pries
her legs apart like an unruly poem
swarming in a reader's shallow breath
meant to seduce her. She is controlled
by what she sees. On the altar
in the corner an icon is shy
as if by accident—these things
are unfashionable but work. She prays
to St. Hardwork St Lucky St Chicago
& rests on her heels as she prays,
later, still in the glow of the electric heater,
before she subsides into the wary bed.

The political radio plays music
for her & her sister, the words
have nothing to do with the music—
she lingers at the beach, a black
face full of compassion comes close,

a tongue licks her breast, the news
comes on & no one listens, the sisters
are snoring, angels cluster
where virgins sleep, did you know that,
they ward, they kiss & clip, they hanker
& move the astral forms of the sleepers
towards innocent catastrophes of lust,
their thighs opening soft as snowfalls.

She came into being
from the book she was reading.

The Devotees

Till in the domestic fire the Sultan saw
his own heart sealed in light

he did not believe the stone that crumbled
or the crystalline sand it became.

"Time should have no sway with me at all
because I am a lover, & that process never ends,

I can never reach finish so I last
as the swiftest of the slow who hurry there."

Was anybody listening? Did the sky care
how many lovers or sleepers rolled below it?

"We are the clouds of the mind. From us
the weather of time takes its direction,

bringing storms to town or ships to safe harbor.
Why am I the only one who loves?"

Then they split open the fire & showed light,
slit the light open & showed his human heart.

"You are right," they told him, "you alone
from the beginning of the world, only You."

Day 5-Quiej

Day of what is big on four feet
big as a man but a man
is not afraid of it: that animal
whichever it is.
Only of it
a man
is not afraid.
The soft animals
the ponies the bambis.

These are the persons
who learn to talk; listen
to the cantilena in the underbrush,
the horses are talking,
those hard-foot invaders. "We

brought the white men.
When you see one of them
he is always on us or on wheels
that go as we taught him to go.
We brought him here."

And back in the forest by the green water
looks like jade in the rainy light

the deer people are weeping & scheming.
They say: "We will lead

———

*Quiej is a Day God in the calendar of the Quiché of Highland Guatemala.
Dennis Tedlock tells me that* quiej *originally meant 'deer,' then after the
Spaniards came turned to mean 'horse.'*

190

him to the ocean of dream,
we will whisper his fear
will break him. His fear

will take him & his horses away."

Early Spring Day Along the Housatonic

To John Ashbery

Water the quick anemone. We flower.
There was a sheer oil like rain
on the soft clean machinery.
It was the Derby Dam two months ago,
the river of such associations
lovely cold the timid bungalows
below the sluiceway, wide channel
for summer but there were no boats
though the last of March it had been 90.

Too many details. There's a library
where all this is stored. Woodstock
where it's cooler. The dam controls
were navy grey spelt gray. The road
ran by the river then crossed the dam
narrow, a diphthong. Thirty years ago
one would have thought of sabotage.
Now her feet are free of shoes,
zori on the car floor but her shapely
feet are naked on the controls.

Soon the houses would be opened up
smelling of winter and linoleum.
The old tv still seems to work
—only channels 3 and 8. The rain
presently is washing blue rooves—
gummy kind of shingle, tar-like,
gulls sit there often. Wood
has been so good to us all these
hundred hundred thousand years.

But in Woodstock even the old are young
and no one admits. *Ne passera*
they have been crying forty years.
Even the young are. The sad cocaine.
The library's books are old too,
expensive art books locked
away in a grilled-door manger.
I'm always 5 years old when I walk in
gulpy and foolish, awk and ward
since the alternative is to be
a ponderous half-celebrity, a poet

or other unreal river dammed
a few civil minutes so I dont drown
these competent handsome librarians.
I think about the rain in Derby
(here it is midnight, Hudson, dry)
and a daylight building in Woodstock
across the street from the laundromat.
If I try to read my eyes keep staring
out at the wash being tumbled forever

around and flop around and flop I'm down
at the bottom of the page without a clue.
I am as bad as a politician glad with names
or I am a pelican who eats all manner
fish. Mountain, river, dam,
the spindly, oily, navigable rain.
Dont you find it lonely with
all and only those memories? I do.
Consider the bungalow a-port
of the one futzing outboard moving

against the shore where taxes live.
There are people now say in New Haven
who'll come up open your door soon,
house. Ice-box will not smell bad.
There is a dead rat under the stove.
The mayonnaise jar full of plastic spoons
promises its own kind of welcome.
There is a piano. She sits down
horrified to be here again. Her father

is talking to the dog. Her hands reflect
hours applied to Mozart and Bach.
It makes the dog nervous mother thinks.
A walk is gone for, the piano
is returned to, supper is brought in—
a huge flat square cardboard box.
The love that bonds them here is real,
it is our only real religion
and sometimes I think it is our only love.
It trusts the orderly power of dams

up to and not including dreams.
When it is night the father sleeps
back at his desk at the Press,
sometimes his secretary undresses him
reverently caressing his socks.
He half-wakes and groans and turns.
The dreams of a mother are vivid and sad,
full of premiums unpaid, wallpaper
crawling to the floor. Never will she tell.

But the pianist who has been
dreaming all day is used up by midnight.
She curls in a ball. The dog.
The brother arrives from Cambridge
addled with dope, he sleeps
on the sunporch davenport, the dog
is continually disturbed. Night,
but I mention no names. Cartoon
of lovers, families, houses. Why
not believe the dream is solid and holds?

Because the spillway runs all day
all right. Some fine day will break:
anyone can tell that just by looking.
At anything. Rain so soft
the windows seem surprised, undone.
A bowl of eggs on the oilcloth'd table,
organic, bought from the farmer.
At some point in the night everyone
worries about the boat. Mother

hopes soon to eat a lobster.
Brother is learning Chinese.
Some nights she prays the dog will die,
her father is so lonesome with it.
He is lost out there now, his boss's hand
easy on the back of his neck, feel
of a warm dishcloth loving him. He whimpers.
She hates the piano. She hopes he
will stop using that stuff, those things.
He hopes the weekend passes fast.

It is not that men are frightened of the rain.
The bridge it first looks like is stalwart,
everything can cross. It is not that thinking
is difficult; it is so sensual to think
that most people are afraid of it.
You cant think without skin, lung, heart—
that is the mystery. I doubt very much
there's a book in the library that doesnt say so.
It is not that mystery itself is terrible

but men who have mysteries to disclose
are pompous and awful. Dont believe them
except when they talk about machinery
or sometimes the rain, or times when they remember
who played left field for the Boston Braves
or what happened to whom when the river rose
before the dam was ever built and houses,
cars and cows swept down into the Sound
with empty mayo jars bobbing in the surf.
Last year's flies likewise come back to life.

But in Woodstock what would I gather?
A hook for her hair. A book
to lie on her other side at night
to shape the imaginative breeze.
Some nutritious tao fu not to overdo.
Turkish apricots. Pistachios.
Technical reports on dbX's.
Details "without significance"
the pastor said, "beatnik bluff,

hedonistic precisions, soft junk."
I could almost believe he had suddenly
seen through the rain. Some orange honey.
Across the street the Christian Science church
surrounds itself with little woods
right there on the main drag, "no priest
but the perfected man." The rain
over Connecticut was true, blue
grey dam wheels and gears, tubs and ladders,
could have been anywhere at all

where the beautiful intelligence of men
commands a river. A book. A bungalow.
Old Scott's catalogue, stamps of Ingermanland,
Obock, Montenegro. Magazines
to read while you wait for the Book to open,
the sun stream down Tinker Street and hard
driving rain beat past in, the devil
abusing his wife, the wind up on Mead's
Mountain disguised as an Indian:

"I owned all this junk once, even the blue
grey paint on the battleships. I kissed
it goodbye as the expression goes.
I like to hear her play *Carnaval*,
fat march at the end of it. Beauty
is the one thing that is not opinion.
For its sake I let everything go. It fell
32 feet per second per second down past Canopus
where the imaginal world of my motherfather
hums in the dreams of rainsoaked pilgrims."

It is formal, it is perfectly willing
to end the way ordinary things do.
The librarian holds a book on her lap.
The brother wakes up before anybody.
"From the Housatonic to the Hudson once
all one nation," he remembers
and stares at the uncooperative river, clear
boundary of nothing at all. The gulls
are pawky. But the boats are awake.

The Ones

who come
to help us
will not
look like strangers,
will not seem
like ancestors
come back

will not look
like the pictures
in our temples,
those fingerprints,
relics, foot-
marks saved by priests.

They will look
like ourselves,
in no way
discriminable
to the senses.
To learn to love them,
love us.
They come
in us.

If they look strange and wonderful, they're Hudsons and Cortezes and slavers. He will come back looking as he always did, a man mistakable for other men, not splendid. He did not ripple with siddhis and power—many scoffed. He was not conspicuous—Judas had to point him out to the arresting officers. He was nothing to look at.

Stars?

He'll look
like a candle
cheap paraffin
groped for & lit
when all power fails.

Casting

I was close
to the moon

I mean I fell
for every option

*

("To evoke Dionysus scares up a flight of shadows."
　　　　　　　—Hillman, *Myth of Analysis*, 266.)

What falls
when a stone
is thrown
at sunset
is more than one
sun. Its shadow
sails along the gold
grass of evening
& joins its primary
suddenly,
　　　　　at a place
we call There,
that's where the stone fell.

*

One God
with many shadows.

*

Or, drifting
off to sleep:

The sun *is*
Her shadow.

Ghazal

Are there at evening shuddering palaces
Where among shadows the moths go broke for light

Is there a broken shutter banging in the wind
Or is she just a breeze in a book?

But nice feral muscles of the sumac night play
Let lovers whisper among the transistors—

Under noise a continent of calm goes on
Right at the core of the clatter of hardware.

We are tender in the treasuries of tomorrow,
Our hands caressing switches that speak the light.

≡

"Seven cities
I was born in,
seven have I seen.

A glue
boiled from the skin
of seven animals
holds me to the world

I dangle
from an equinox
neither fully an adherent of the Text
nor yet a castaway"

he speaks of himself
in seven languages
his cat
has only seven lives

seven rivers
irrigate his floor
his house
has seven doors
each door
has seven houses
opening from it

each it
has seven wives.

A Book of Solutions

in memory of Louis Zukofsky

O seek
her, need
her
    not
to leave her

we hear in *Tristan*. Somewhere inside, there is a someone who hears everything in his own native language, in American, no matter what "language" is being spoken. This in me hears as American all the Latin my Catholic childhood overswarmed me with, all the Italian and German and Spanish and Yiddish I heard on the street or somehow learned, later, to read. No matter what vocal sounds are made, this *Native Hearer* resolves the noise into local communication.

The poet's problem and solution: keeping in touch with the Native Hearer. LZ, in composition and translation, single-tongued showed the way.

And to grieve for him I hear:

Day is a ray, day is ill of
Solve it, seek land
In farewell-her.
Test a day with come: she wills it.
Wants us, tremor, lust for you is
Want, o you Text. Her venture is
Cunt, her strict discussion! Yours!
To be mirror-sparse in sunlight!

Swallowtail

I prayed to her

to save me
she sent

a butterfly a black
one with salmon coral
spots on underwings,
their tops extended
white-spot rimmed
& in the black center a
fan of cerulean blue

it let me stand
above it ten minutes
watching it quiver
while it did what?

what do souls do?
mostly close
sometimes spread open
that summer sky
it held in its black wings

1.

Not stealthily,
surefooted, slow
I approached
over gravel
the beautiful

black lace flitter
had come by & rested
on a mud slick
beside the lawn,
with the strangest
confidence
in bright sunlight
I stepped close
till I stood above it
knowing

2.

It was my soul
to which I had come
when I needed one

this dark short-lived
victim of transformation
into the bright air

beads of coral on its wing,
of white & citrine—
let the sun fade

(the sun faded) this
is mine, nervously
frightened & almost

taking flight but not quite
whenever I moved my arm
—the soul dreads bodies

warned me
of such appetency
but did not fly

3.

What it was doing
was unknown to me.

The repertory
of my understandings
was smaller

than the repertory of
its gestures. Sex
Feeding   Excretion
I could understand
but it had no sex

it didnt eat, it hovered
in the world & let
nothing out, it moved

in one place, did not
travel except
through all the countries
of itself ascending
or going down

4.

Madness is homecoming.
Frail wreath
of earthly pleasures
my body of use
only to follow.

Stand here outside
celebrate
in the universal Alone

where no one is
but by being
is in touch

with everyone who ever is.

5.

And I had prayed
knowing nothing
but the insoluble
hungers of my natural
part

    to which she sent
not answers but
a butterfly
as-is

bright on the rim of the mind.

Tannhäuser

        The Pope *is* Queen Venus
When She forgives you he

the branch
flowers
        the dead branch
                        blossoms,
    the mort imagination
                    puts words out again
he "sings"

                    *

the dead imagination
forsythia
        Bronx Parkway
    early in
April
        one year in March,
Co-Op City. Persephone.

                    *

When he was a young knight
still at morning feeling
that innocent upsurge from mulacakra
still touched by the wet daffodils
some doll gave him he spreads
the petals of & sighs inside, spreads
& wants to penetrate, sighs, sports
behind the ear greased by her time.

                    *

His music
got so intricate
it led
him deep into
(if in it is)
the mountain
of his mind
where he found
Women
energetic
whose Behavior
was absolute.
They were ultimates, crazed
to serve his pleasures
at what he took to be his wish.

He accepted them
as his environment
& remained.

                              *

Men said: These are not
real women, these are
only. Only in your
head.

     Their merely
disgusted him.
His mind, so energetic so
musical, was better far
than that simple rumored 'real'

his colleagues babbled of,
drunk sailors
remembering sleazy islands.

*

Yet when he believed them
the wood turned green in his hand.

The Shortstop

Pick up the ball and hold it
while you analyze the vectors
of the heart. To describe
for the fullest time this town
knowing where every street goes
and who lives there. And why.
Where does the money come from?
The old house on the corner
has been painted brown.
Your dog never came home.
To analyze the spaces
inside a broken house. To touch
her again where she's softest,
most impossible to describe.
To find all the mythologies
her name opens up, to enter
that museum or laboratory
or bedroom or terrible porch
on a summer sunset there is
no one at all in the street.
Throw the batter out.

The Trial

1.

Near the touch to complain
it was not so. Not a sound.
How she heaved herself up
as if what I was watching
was worth watching.
North of here, a road
that twisted, similarly.
Narrow voice of her eyes
abolish. Something like blue.

A floor a dance.

2.

The smooth or prelude
to twisty music stung
basely on the floor—
certain arches
reinterpreted as written text
to puzzle us survivors.
The plane I was
had crashed in her loinlands—
my brutal fantasies
battled in a country
stony as Saturday.
Some few were caring. These
I exhibited in my defense.

3.

I was on trial for her trail.
I had pursued the thought of her
till I couldnt get away.
I had paid music. Pronouns
crystallized in the blue soup
softly. I could blur my hands.
Ego cold at the heart, a meat
hung on a hook, a getting
ready but never being there.

4.

Now only it was clear how
legal the definitions
of my more and more abstract
desire had become. Sapphire
I couldnt at the moment afford.
The best was a book
stuck in the wall like a rat
afraid to leave utterly
this choice carrion of a house.
Eat me. Subsume
my starry liquor
in your strong mouth.
Swallow like spitting me out.

5.

What was it a table
a book of Céline a leaf

amputated from this linden
a horse on Sunday
passing, all the black riders.
I felt wedged in the world
& kindly as stars
festooned in my brutal zodiac
waiting for her.
All enough or half for you
to do, exactly, hurry
my moiety, part
my rancid sea.

6.

But it was sapphire, was
fire. Crotch of a tree
I found it, left from Egypt:
humans are from contour
formed, but in this kingdom
men make contours—
this land is a machine.
The sex will never leave you
no matter how you worship
history. The gods will never silence
themselves in your reach.
Your flesh was message, fool,
and reminiscence. It was fur
or a walled city or a box
containing what cannot be contained.

A New Ecology

This man is feeding birds
by living minute to minute.
He thinks. He throws his life
away, where the gull sees it,
where it has so little meat
even the gulls dont eat, dont sink
down to speculate
these weird bones.
If we died they would not mourn us
but they would be less.
The relation between us
(built on complementary appetites)
is incomprehensible and permanent.
This is the future of the world,
already an unreadable history.

The Shield of Achilles

shows a eucalyptus capsule (called "button")
and a button from my favorite shirt, blue
flowers in vertical bands, blue sky sown (sémé)
on the ground. A vertical music is heard
by mourning shepherds ("Linos!") at the city gates
near the Zoo that spreads out around them darkly
beastly voices out of undergrowth. A tree
bonsai'd in terra cotta, its growth made curt
like the breath of a dying man. *Love made
this gate* beyond all dying, let human praise
open the lock. All praise is reverence enough.

Then there's a shape like a television screen
that pictures too small a part of something for
us to tell what the whole thing is. A mountain
on fire? Clamped jaws of a mountain lion?
It tells us (or tries to) what the day is. Not even fire
can obliterate what we learn from it:

There is a window in the fact of things—from
it we see a street, a girl calls certain words
in a high incomprehensible street vibrato
gaily to friends. She names a god and flees in
hope he'll follow. She is the picture, going.
Around that single image the nervous world
imagines itself compelled to grow, become
a place for her to run through. We
are the shadow of her flight. This dense
exile seizes us and makes us stay.
The images, vague as someone else's meaning,
glow in the worked electrum. A picture of God

is what it is. Some ordinary thing
just as it is, irreducible. Nothing
can conquer the hero who holds it in his hands.

Her Name

Am) I a civil
war does it touch
me where do you
live most
beautiful harlot
I followed
you were) my mother)
ica.

This Earth a Necklace Bead for Whom

"This earth a necklace bead for whom?
Pierced in her? Centered?"
It is centered.
We make it wobble
but it rights itself. Always.
We are Juan and Consuela,
we are Nuestra Señora de Merced,
we are in a corner, by the cactus
in the cartoon, asleep.
The Blessed Mother stands before us
Her lap full of roses
or She is bleeding.
The frail flowers of time She pours
into our eternal silence.
We are me. We are America.
Men give milk—
after the beginning
She needs this food.
A vulture prances on a skull,
tourists pass, their simple hearts
greedy for experiences.
I kneel in the road
pretending to an assassination,
the Virgin presses Her rose against me
while all the cars overheat.
The rain alone heals our situation.
Later under my blanket I find stars
signalling to me
from what I had thought was a private dark.
She whose least concern is our wet earth
is with me everywhere, Her messages naked.

You Are in Water

You are in water now
the twine of midnight
strung around your feet

It is sleep

There is a number
leads you inward

With bare feet
you step ashore.

Will you remember the touch of the boat, the water up to your knees, your throat welcoming the terrors of America, canoe, raft, mastodon, white whale? Nine men were here before you, they are dead.

Your grandfather is dead. Who will teach the owl to understand what you say? The eagle sits by the fire. It is old and you are young, you catch fish but the fish are old. Not even the water. You age to eat. It is cold. I cant understand what you're saying, are they words? Cold moons. Mouth your way to noon. Now who listens?

Their bones are everywhere, the clouds shunt above them to comment on their fall. Who were these people of whom you are never a descendant? You are exact and new, hence you are silent.

There was no one before. You are your mother swung from the birthpost on her desolate night you come forth.

The Lover

Now then or the white spirit
spoke language in her clothes:

Tomorrow, by the water-fountain
they call it, the tennis cage, noon or four.

"When you have gone to a strange city
I will count things till I forget"

and so our meeting place is waste. A man
without an elephant, alive, in shadow,

hears for example owls there. O love
when you shall have gone to a northern city

I shall finger myself for days afraid of strangers.
Then the tree will open. The voices

I banished into wood will croak and hiss,
none of them will pronounce your name.

The park will leave me then,
birds will hold their congress on my steps

and as I mount the spattered staircase morning
love will point out an inevitable stranger

to be seen if I just turn my graceful head.
There he is, among the chrome and fenders

articulate the minute he sees my face.
Love is good for him too I fancy.

With a mouth full of sweet precisions
he hurries towards me through the scattering doves.

The Goddess

the vine
interprets her feet
going make ground
"infer

yourselves, humans,
I speak.
Intuit
lanterns,

lakes, fine books,
things armed,
owned, warm
hands,

securities,
each
generation will increase.
Imagine

propagation. Exalt
yourselves
with proliferation.
Enjoy the plumbing.

Every hair breathes.
Every star
breeds
resemblances.

I sound so cold
to make you

doubt
my beauty

that relentless
quality
that persists
beyond

your certainty.
What is known
is noble.
What forgets,

forgives."

The Visit

Filled with a curious ecstasy she discovers
a hut in the forest covered with dead leaves.
To her knock nothing but a bird or scuttling
sounds in the leaves. "Who is there?" she asks
as if she were the visited interior. No answer
relieves her embarrassment. "Why have I come?
Is there anybody I really want to know?" Silence.

Then there was a man regarding her from nowhere,
she could not place his ground, he fascinated her
briefly by his independence of being anywhere at all.
He was firm but shadowy, his voice was heavy,
as if he lifted it from that same uncertain floor.
"I will tell you why you've come. I have called you
by speaking into my own bones, my deft fingers

found you between my thighs, and pulled you, slow
as flowers are supposed to grow, down into this daylight.
I am the unreliable one in the heart of the wood—
come give me pleasure." His thick meaning
moistened itself then in her mouth. He too was from heaven,
was waiting for the earth to open at last, to be done
with it. To be done with it forever, and go home.

Portrait of a Man Alone

She walks along the tundra of his mind
a satisfying reindeer dance, albino
under the heavy creamy stars, a walk
of a naked foot elegantly stepping
not altogether trusting the soft ground.

Her soft ground. And where he should be babbling
about the perfection of her Urn, turn
of her buttock and dense juices of her Door,
he worries the morality of heaven.
Would Krishna do this, or Christ, or Shiva?
The love that meant to worship turns to mind.
But that is after all the place she dances.

The Dismembered

The sex they do against me in the streets leaves me poor as a star in the attics of a painful century. "Better century," I hear you say, but you forget anaesthesia. You forget radio—which is good, it frees, it frees most people from that burden of incessant telepathy which is mine. My burden is your mind, dont you know that? Sometimes I'm glad to bear.

How they choose anyone but me makes them eccentric, me mad, mad to care, crazy, cold as a fish, full of monsters I am slated to become. I burn with desire, and have since my seventh year, I am a prodigy of claim upon, upon all your beauty. You who go to sleep and smile, can you imagine the need that never sleeps, that slakes itself with excess and austerity and denial all, no difference, the orgy or the cellula alone, can you, what it means, when, the mind itself is burning?

These poets who translate horror from language to language! Safe in the non-committal zoo of surrealism, what do they know of the dark? The dark is not some logical proposition to be couched in these terms or those. The dark is the absence of propositions. The dark is not an image, convenient, a commodity that like a quarter adds up in some pig bank.

It is a crucifixion where you are the Christ and you dont believe in Christ but why are you hurting? The dark is not something to sell, to translate from French into what you think is American but is the foul syntax of inattention. The dark is not Spanish, not a lemon at midnight or to sit on a wall still warm from the sun. There never was any sun but me in this universe. These vile poets who think the dark is something to say! It is a muscle that squeezes us out and sometimes we cry and sometimes the cry's a word. And sometimes not.

Virgil

If Virgil this jet heard breaking what would he the air
think here of our poor haunted footsteps
from candle faltering to candle in the temple
he never knew the god's name of it he never
a sense of its precinct measured his our hope
moving by night. Enough poor child says he your sky breaks
and to what end enquire city you never imagine?

The Place

It was a destiny we used to call it,
waiting for the subway on scuzzy well-made
wooden benches shining in sweat-light, special shabby
low watt bulbs the subway used, sometimes
like remembering a woman in the yuk of the day
sometimes you see a blue one. Get off there
between the stations. There
in summer the sun streams vertically down
shredding the gothic underwear below the city
and we breathe. In winter this
is a warm condition, whose mental inhabitants
burst out of their clothes with longing for you.
The furrow from navel down to business
is a shadow of soft hairs. Stay there.
The destinations any society imposes
are full of shit. The stations. Strike off
into the naked geology of fact. Love all of her
with equal reverence. This dark
means to teach wonder. The inhabitants
are full of wonder and they share. They breathe
intelligently in the foul air and never care.
They take you to their laps with equal reverence.
What you thought was a train buzzes in your head.

"Queen of Heaven" Variations

on a poem by N.N.

The locations or
coming back on it again, "Queen of Heaven"
a vessel chartered out of these seas
no port into a sudden calm above all water

she holds,
            blue-masted, stretched
out over the palpable,
                        in command
that we, out of the city I stand ever in, reach
up to touch
            her and not touch,
her condition eludes
the rafters of my house I see her
there are no rafters, the roof
is a dome and send every message
to,
    there are shad in the river,
and eels, and turreted sturgeons
                        horny with roe
move in her company,
                assumed
with her into our heavenheads,
                        cherishing.

She who had been a mother rose
like a fat-bottomed boat now
billowing into the creamy air
where her son Daylight
waits with His dark Father,

her masts crack, bones
give away their mortal salve
    mid-air shipwreck, keel
does what?
        drops
  down and splits our old heads
lets this new sky in,
         the vast
body her wood body has become
outward travelling,
        stars,
pores of her now unending skin.

Herod

Her back is forth and I have tasted every music.

Her ass is full of reminiscence, she carries
disordered wine in a black gold cup squeezed
between her thighs and knees, the grapes
grew in a crazy summer, crows died on my vines

and this is their too sweet Saturnian wine.
My passion will drink her, passion
lives lonely in my eyes."

        The courtiers
turned him then and aimed him at the dark.

INRI

for M.S.

No crooning over spoiled miles
weird milk
keening up her arm
a lost
smoothness where the spikes ran in
she knew
the agony her body
was the garden she lay
three days nodding in the tomb.

Seeds

In desire tunes a lotus fix the world.
Whatever tongue I speak speaks to me,
sometimes in me, the syllable /aː/
lights up in the balmy moon,
cream of underpants and ordinary woe
peppering that winsome face, bowl
of our paranoid arrivals. Then
let that turn to a blue flower
much sought after, rested on, a beamy
lunacy on the lady's face who squats
panting Saturn's opium in, black
sequences, black octaves, till
the syllable /tãː/ appears on the petal
closest to zenith. Then the smoke
clears, she looks out on the snow
being a sacred person, yes, and being separate.
No newspaper in sight, sign of an early time.
Prayerflags. Saturn is Siva. Growth
is form. New day new god. Fidelity
to the darkest cameras of saying so,
this speech my heartbeat and burnt offering.

≡

The holy mist
with sun gone up in it
look
there might be two advancing,
Dante, a woman with him,
whose description
parses and abolishes our condition

Where the roads divide
they scrutinize
the delicate choices
left them by their sins.
This might be eternity, a slow
dance they try to remember
as they tried
even there, in mist, to
remember weather.
How long since they were bodies.
Once she had drunk too much
and wet her clothes—isnt that
love also, isnt that a root
holds us in the world?
It had been long.
                        She could remember
her thighs, how they parted
for glory after glory
(as she thought of them, those dome-
building orgasms of light
her husband seeded in her—
and what did he have
to do with her dour companion
now? who walked with her

because of love, a passion
that—like their God—
was word.)

What does it feel like to be flesh?
"We who are exalted"
she began, and he, having lifted
his heart so often to that altar
bowed his head. "My dear,
my dearest, what is there to say?"
But again she offered: "We
who are exalted
falter
sometimes in a dream of light.
Then a dark
that is God
comes down
and we walk
among Him as once
once we walked so happily,
so seldom together,
the filth that is life.
God between our toes!"
He smiled at her,
his lovely heretic
almost, his pantheist,
the mist so lucid now
her face was part of it.
After so many years
when her face was the whole
to which every other percept was
part or beggary or patch.

Where the roads divide
they walk
apart into their worship
having been perfect
to each other.
She goes, lifting her voice often,
through this mystery that is morning.
And he has found his silence in her at last.

The Death of Lenny Bruce

Smooth face of another country
where men wake happy
from an unmeasuring sleep.
They get up from the tile floor
and there are deserving Maidens who
forgive the clotted
blood off their arms with tongues.
What time is it? he wants to know.
Time for a Mars bar, a scalene
wedge of chocolate sticks to his right pap—
I'm due in Montreal. This is Montreal.
It is snowing. This is Canada. This is surely
Philadelphia it is snowing. It is Miami.
The Civil War statues are wet with smiles.
I'm due in Washington. It is snowing
on the libraries with needles,
there is a white building where they wait for me
this word I have for them you hear.
They get up from the tile floor like a litany.
What a strange religion it is to be dead.
It is not as one expects. "To begin with,
it is like Montreal, elegant, familiar,
a strange language is common. There is snow.
I know that without opening my lids. I'm too tired
to fuck anybody and that seems to be permitted,
my image they tell me is intact. Everywhere
I expected anguish, but there was audient silence
then sweet applause. The stone smiles all round me.
One of these minutes I'm going to open my eyes."

It Is Always a Matter of Return

It is always a matter of return. Who had come
from the dark beaches of Canarsie
where the drenched sand looked volcanic,
obsidian pulverized by giant children
seeing Unity behind the obvious
trinitarian mysteries of sea and shore—see Augustine.
Who came up from the mountain outside Juarez
baked in complex sunlight, the kind
northern tourists are always trying to buy.
Or the blue mountain in the Laramies
that suddenly meant one thing: Make
love to me here, this summit. And there
for once she would not. It's just a matter
of timing. There are days when even
I don't want to read Augustine, watch the sea,
walk on the beach, make love, say the word
'obsidian.' Such days are few but they do come,
once in a calendar. And then it's a matter of wanting
to be around the corner from myself
not mapped into routines. There must
be a city for those days too, full of
strangers who only look like us, smiling, chewing gum.

≡

Say good morning to the earliest machine
"fable of our separateness," who speaks?
Alone with the lupine, mountain man.
And in the peat pot the sleeping amaryllis
dreams crimson eternities,
phalluses tender and rigid, both are sweet,
to lift into the morning. Shiva's ice lingam
melts in the womb of the day. Go soft
young man and she will love thee,
exerting her own power to lift you both
—that is how yearning is best satisfied,
when the man sleeps and the woman labors
making the mill turn round the stone.

Printed November 1979 in Santa Barbara & Ann Arbor
for the Black Sparrow Press by Mackintosh and Young
& Edwards Brothers Inc. Design by Barbara Martin.
This edition is published in paper wrappers; there
are 250 hardcover copies numbered & signed by the
author; & 50 numbered copies have been handbound in
boards by Earle Gray, each containing an original
ink drawing and holograph poem by the author, from
the Second Series of the *The Mirsuvian Calligraphies*.

Photo: Richard Gummere

Everything that ought to be known about Robert Kelly can be found in his books, of which this is the fortieth. The long poem *The Loom* (1975), the collection of poems *Flesh Dream Book* (1971), *The Mill of Particulars* (1973), *Kali Yuga* (1970) and *The Convections* (1978) he regards as especially relevant, along with the essays called *In Time* (1971) and the long poem about America called *The Common Shore* (1969 etc.). Recently published have been an allegorical text in three measures, *The Cruise of the Pnyx* (1979) and a sequence *The Book of Persephone* (1978). Soon to be published is an examination of Irish-American excuses called *Erin Tantra America*. He lives in Upstate New York and teaches writing at Bard College.